Thierry Bouët
Hotel People

Foreword by Pino Cacucci

Smithsonian Institution Press
Washington, D.C.

Originally published in Italian in 1996
by Federico Motta Editore

Published 1999 in the United States of America
by Smithsonian Institution Press
in association with Federico Motta Editore, Milan

Translation from Italian by Renata Treitel

Library of Congress Cataloging-in-Publication Data

Bouët, Thierry.
[Gente d'albergo. English]
Hotel people / Thierry Bouët ; text by Pino Cacucci.
p. cm. — (Motta fotografia)
ISBN 1-56098-855-X (alk. paper)
1. Portrait photography. 2. Hotels Pictorial works.
3. Bouët, Thierry. I. Title. II. Series: Motta fotografia
(Washington, D.C.)
TR680.B59 1999
779'.2'092—dc21 99-24730

06 05 04 03 02 01 00 99 5 4 3 2 1

Printed by Arti Grafiche Motta, Milan
Manufactured in Italy, not at government expense

Hotel People

Hotels have layered souls, thin veils of impalpable memory, one for each fragment of life that leaves a trace there. The hotel walls absorb voices, sounds, rustlings, the clicking of keys, sighs, imprecations before the blank sheet or score, shouted arguments, and conspiratorial whispers.

The wallpaper, the wood of the furniture, the ceiling plaster could narrate the genesis of immortal novels, or a good part of the history of jazz as well as that of rock, or the encounter of persons from whom unforgettable events might have sprung: great film, a musical piece destined to echo in every corner of the planet, but also actions hatched in the most absolute anonymity, like a homicide capable of changing the life course of a portion of mankind, or even the beginning of a revolution. The hotel walls become imbued with innumerable lives of which they retain the memory: apparently they are silent guardians, but they are other than blind or deaf.

If there were a magic able to squeeze the soul of the Chelsea Hotel, for example, transforming it into sounds and images, we could relive the creative splendors and the deep human misery of luminous though ephemeral meteors, like Edie Sedgwick, Andy Warhol's model, who twice set this hotel, already scarred by burns, on fire: the Chelsea, magnanimous, kept the fire to itself and guarded, no one knows how, the lunar and ethereal body of Edie, careless smoker and irreplaceable muse.

In the heart of Havana, the Hotel Ambos Mundos resists hurricanes and the saltiness of the sea. It is the only hotel that knows *For Whom the Bell Tolls.* Hemingway lived there for months and years. In 1939 in those rooms he heard again the voices of Maria and the *Inglés,* Pilar's laughter, the din of the war, and the silences of the blood-covered mountains, until, having reached the last page, he heard, with his ear touching the floor of the Ambos Mundos, the heart of Robert Jordan beating "against the pine needle floor of the forest." At that moment, he typed "The End" and looked for a large house for himself on top of the hill, the *Finca Vigia,* though nothing would be the same as before.

Hotels are good to put lives into parentheses: they are oases and havens where one can enjoy fully the fleeting time of each day, without letting the thousand duties imposed by a normal existence erode and gnaw it away. Parentheses that open and close as one enters and leaves, protective wrappings for vagabond spirits who find here shelter from the daily magma. The list of famous characters who have chosen a hotel as an abode is infinite, from the most tormented artists to the best-heeled entrepreneurs, in addition to the illustrious nobodies, unknown to the point of preferring a hotel room just to remain so, or simply to entrust others with managing the lesser problems of existence. On the road there was always a hotel for Jack Kerouac, as well as for William Burroughs and Allen Ginsberg. Jean-Paul Sartre and Simone de Beauvoir lived at the Louisiane from 1943 to 1946, perhaps insignificant compared with Coco Chanel's forty years at the Ritz. And hotels, at times, welcome the end of an extreme trajectory, offering a window for Chet Baker to throw himself from or a room for Jim Morrison to vanish from, he who in Paris started on the road that would make him step over the last threshold, as when he went on an intimate pilgrimage to the Hôtel de Lauzun, which Baudelaire and Gautier had transformed into the Hashish Club.

Yes, it would be great magic to give those walls a voice, to make them tell everything. Something, nevertheless, they do narrate. They tell us of guests who go through without leaving a sign, a mood, a small scratch, nothing; and others who engrave, sculpt, move things around, adapting what is around them to their presence, which then will remain indelible, offering the next traveler the desire to rebuild what has been lived there.

The images of Thierry Bouët are the alchemy that make it possible to hear the voices of the hotels. Photographs that transmit to the glance the soul contained within the walls. And as we look, we begin to listen. . . . Exile, first of all. Raymond Eddé in a meeting with other Lebanese exiles in the Hôtel Queen Elisabeth in Paris. That one photo can evoke a kaleidoscope of stories, different in time and in space, but similar in the drama of uprooting. Here the hotel was not a choice, but it remains a symbol of refuge and protection: all the exiles, survivors of collective dramas from every corner of the world, have found in a hotel the first fixed point in their sad flight and have entrusted it with nostalgia, regret, anger, and their need to remember, to oppose the oblivion that envelops human beings, making them invisible, and to cancel the origin of deep tragedies. Exile and hotel: an eternal wavering between rejection and affection, hatred of the imposed distance that, despite themselves, those four walls represent as well as gratitude for the hospitality they provided when outside the world had reached the point of tearing one apart.

"If I used my reason, I should feel no nostalgia for it," an Argentine exile from the late military dictatorship told me, as he pointed to the modest hotel on the *Avenida Insurgentes Norte* in Mexico City. "Yet . . . there's that room there, on the third floor, see? The second window from the corner on the left. A few months ago, I don't know how to explain it, I was walking by, and I entered, just like that, without even thinking, I entered and saw the old doorkeeper again, always the same, who embraced me as if I had been a relative who had emigrated to a foreign country. . . . And tears rolled down my eyes, as if I had revisited the house of my most cherished memories. But certainly it was not a year of beautiful memories, that one. And the small room on the third floor was the only one I could afford. At first, the thought of having escaped from the horror consoled me, but then, as the months went by . . . In short, reason tells me it was a most horrible year. But my instinct, this damned Argentine instinct, for truly only we could have invented the tango, nostalgic and full of regrets as we are . . . in my gut I feel that I left something of myself in this dingy little hotel and of the story that I carry inside. Now that I have a dignified house and work at a newspaper, now that I can afford what, from that window, seemed an unachievable dream . . . each time I have a pretext to do so, I go to a hotel and feel free.

Thierry Bouët also knows how to recount hotel life with subtle irony. The portrait of Mathilda, for example: capturing her from behind as she looks at the external world—different—he immortalizes the sixth feline permanent inhabitant of the now legendary Algonquin Hotel in New York: by chasing rats she wins the right to stay, but the place where she lives has made her famous, leading her to debut in films.

And if some portraits might transmit a sense of solitude instead, to make solitude vanish it is enough to remember where we stand: outside the room there is the microcosm of a hotel, not the desert of a large condominium, where one may feel more alone than in an empty subway car on the last night's run.

Modern apartment buildings represent the most peculiar contradiction of today's society: the forced close proximity of hundreds of people produces isolation and negates relationships. Obviously, it is not a universal rule, but in large urban areas solitude constitutes the norm rather than the exception. "I have lived in a condominium in Brussels for nine years," the American musician Steven Brown, who recently left Europe for Mexico, told me not long ago, "and on leaving, I realized I did not even know my neighbor across from me. Never an exchange of words, an invitation, a spark of curiosity not prompted by distrust. Fear of having one's own vital space, narrow to boot, invaded by an unknown intruder."

Rarity of contacts also depends, of course, on the nature of a nation or even on the customs of one neighborhood compared with another. But, when one talks of a metropolis and the relations among human beings who crowd there, one can end up appreciating hotel life for this reason also: the same staff who takes care of maintenance, of cleaning up, of sorting messages, or of serving drinks, constitutes in itself a presence that makes for community, that supplies the pretext for a person not to surrender to solitude.

Maybe this is the reason why so many hotel owners, after deciding to put the place up for sale, have kept one suite for themselves, like Robert Laurens with the Ambassador in Paris: where else would he find a family as large as this one?

And there are those who remain after having devoted their life without having ever owned it. Mademoiselle Dumont, who we see move away without hurry, as if she were taking a stroll, entered the Hôtel Lutétia at age fourteen, ran it until she retired, and continues to be its "moral guardian," its living memory. The sculptor César, eternal nomad, has spent long periods at the Lutétia, and Françoise Sagan has often chosen it as the place to write her books. For many writers there seems to be no better place than a hotel to give life to the characters of their works. There is no sadness in the image of Mademoiselle Dumont because the Lutétia is her home as well as her story. What sense would it make to leave now?

"My father came as a mining engineer and ended up being a hotelkeeper," the old owner of a small hotel in Santa Rosalia, Baja California, told me. Son of French people who moved to this kind of *finis terrae,* an extreme strip of desert jutting into the Sea of Cortés in the golden era of metallurgical mines, he inherited the hotel and continues to keep it open even though Santa Rosalia is hardly a tourist mecca.

In the square of the tiny town there looms the strangest church in the Americas, created by Eiffel before becoming universally famous for his Parisian tower. Brought here in the hold of a cargo ship and put together in each of its million nuts and bolts, the church represents the past splendor of a forgotten age. "Mornings I lean over the window, look at the church, breathe in the air from the sea, greet the passersby, and . . . begin my day, chasing away the nocturnal ghosts that incite me to leave everything behind as soon as dawn rises. But I will never leave. Because, no matter what, I would go and live in another hotel, and in that case . . . I prefer to stay in my own hotel, where each beam and each brick are my bones and veins."

Monastery, barracks, ship. Somewhat prison, at times, for some people. But one can disembark from or abandon the hotel. Escape, if the pain of existence becomes so oppressive to make a person mistake the room for a cell.

Outside, there is a road. For people like us, it is twice as precious. It offers knowledge, true, direct, unfiltered. And it has so many hotels along its way, each of them ready to reveal a world. A small world, true, direct, unfiltered.

Pino Cacucci
Hotel Marieta
Playa del Carmen, Mexico
February 1996

Photographs

24. Mara Gibbs, singer, Mark Hotel, New York, 1992
25. Diane von Fürstenberg, designer, Carlyle Hotel, New York, 1991
26. Henri Nijdam, editor, Hôtel Raphaël, Paris, 1991
27. Milos Forman, film director, Hampshire House Hotel, New York, 1991
28. Georges Condo, painter, Hôtel Lotti, Paris, 1991
29. Carlo di Palma, photography director, Mayfair Regent Hotel, New York, 1991
30. Raymond Hains, artist, Hôtel Windsor, Nice, 1993
31. Bob Armas, resident, Hôtel le Montreux Palace, Montreux, 1993
32. Della Tamari, practicing lawyer, Parkes Hotel, London, 1992
33–34. Roger Peters, producer, Savoy Hotel, London, 1992
35. Mr. and Mrs. Dracoulis, shipowners, Hôtel Plaza Athénée, Paris, 1991
36–37. Annik Bickson, daughter of the hotel manager, Mark Hotel, New York, 1991
38. Mademoiselle Dumont, former housekeeper of the hotel, Hôtel Lutétia, Paris, 1991

Hotel People

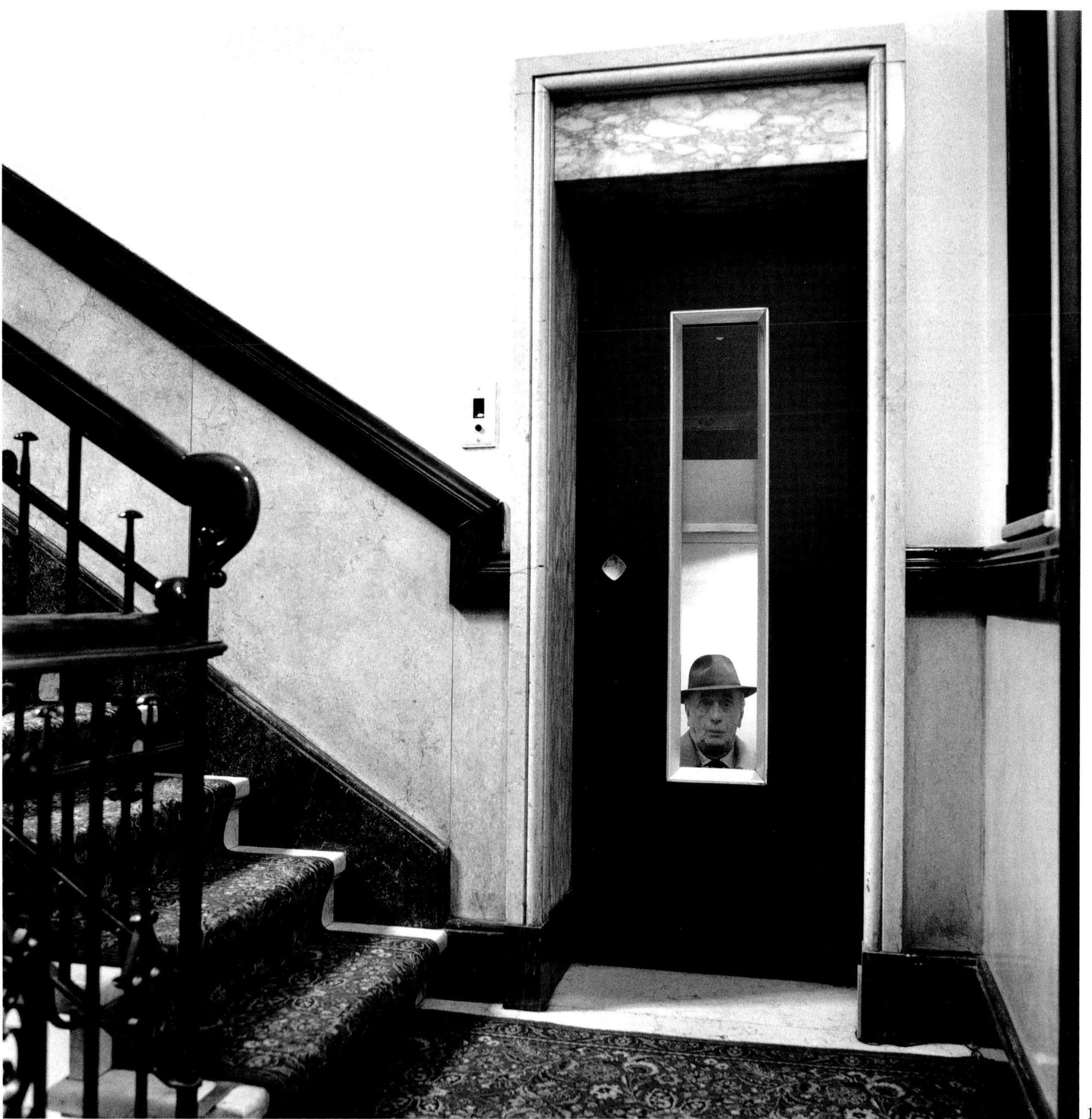

1

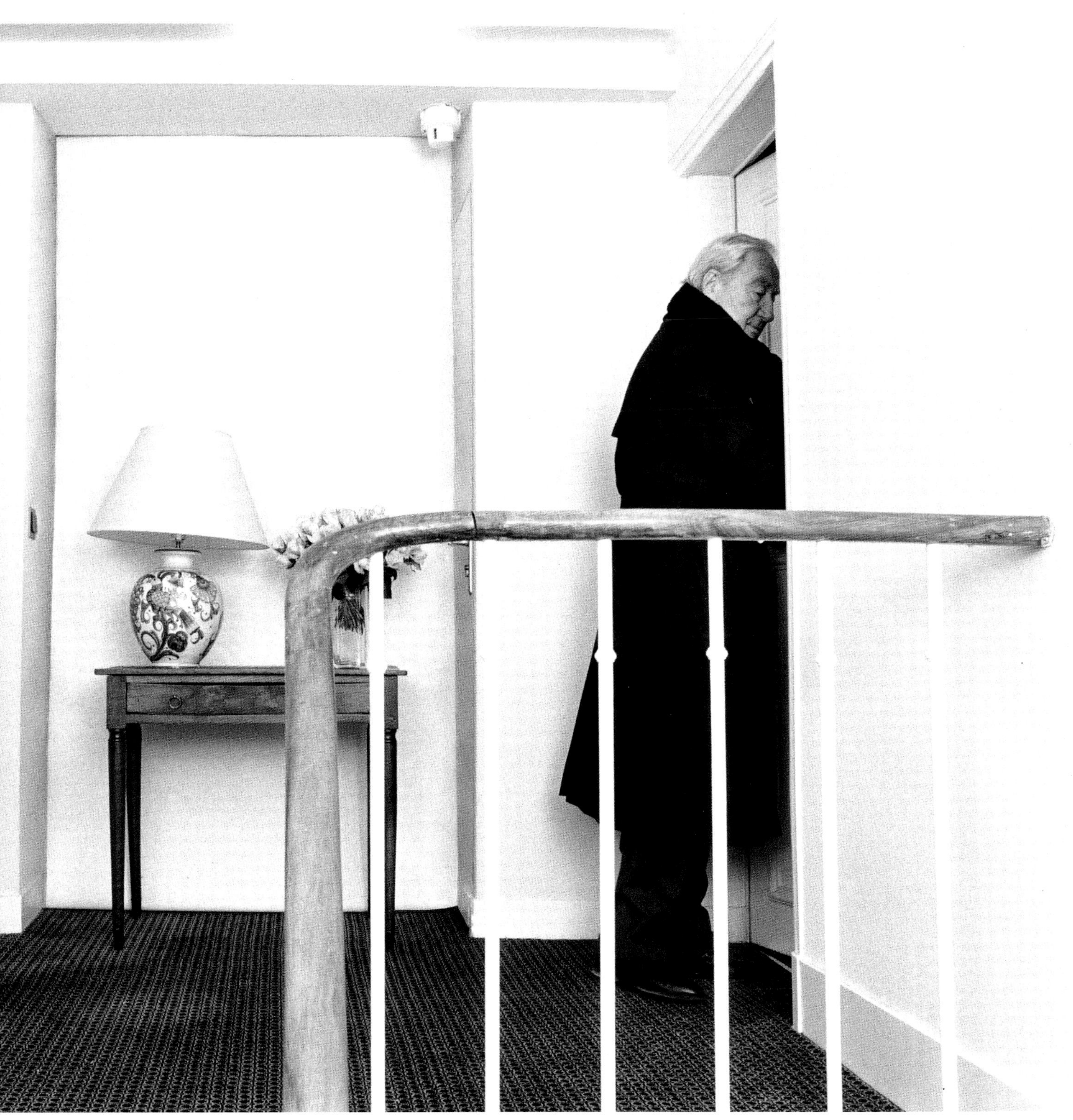

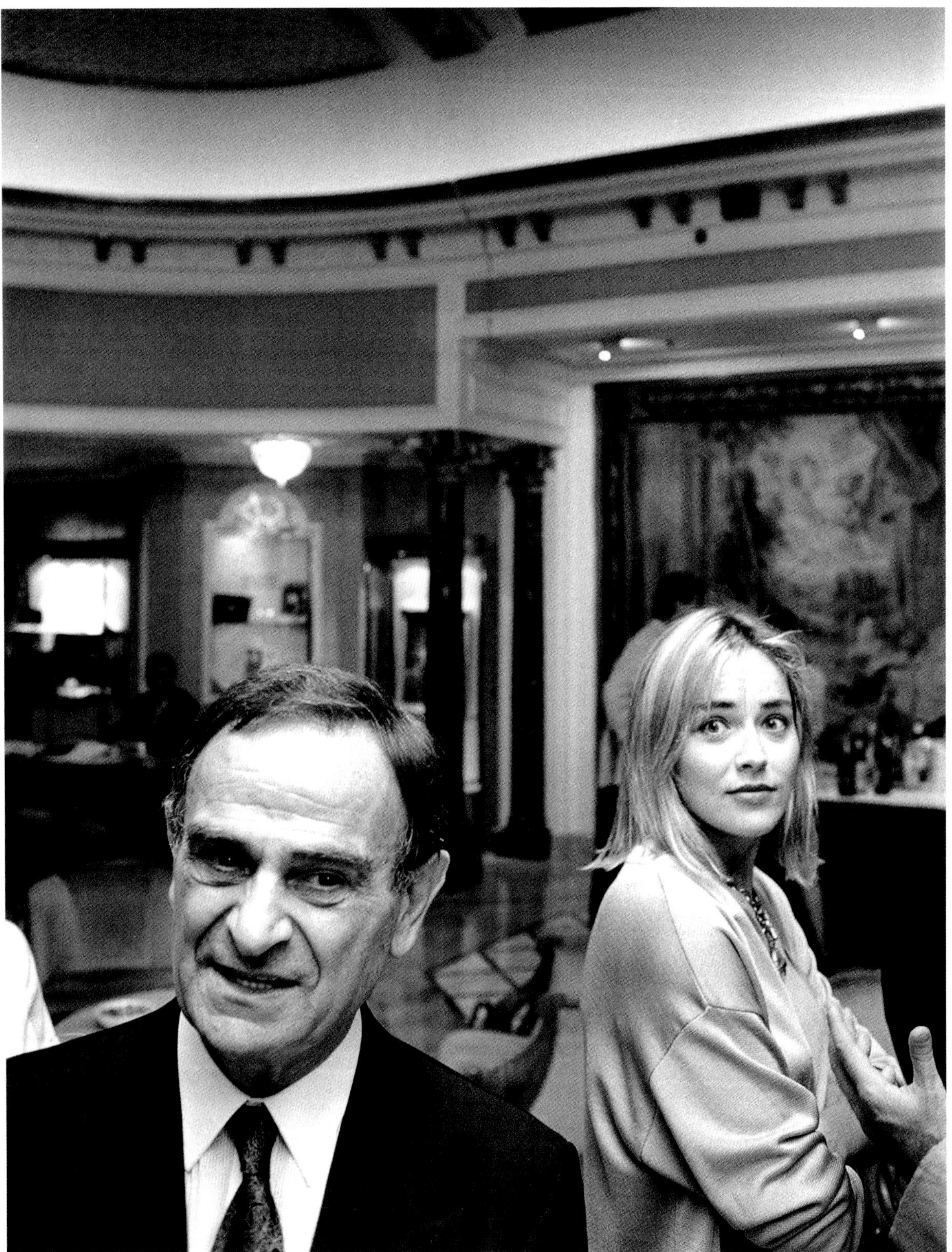

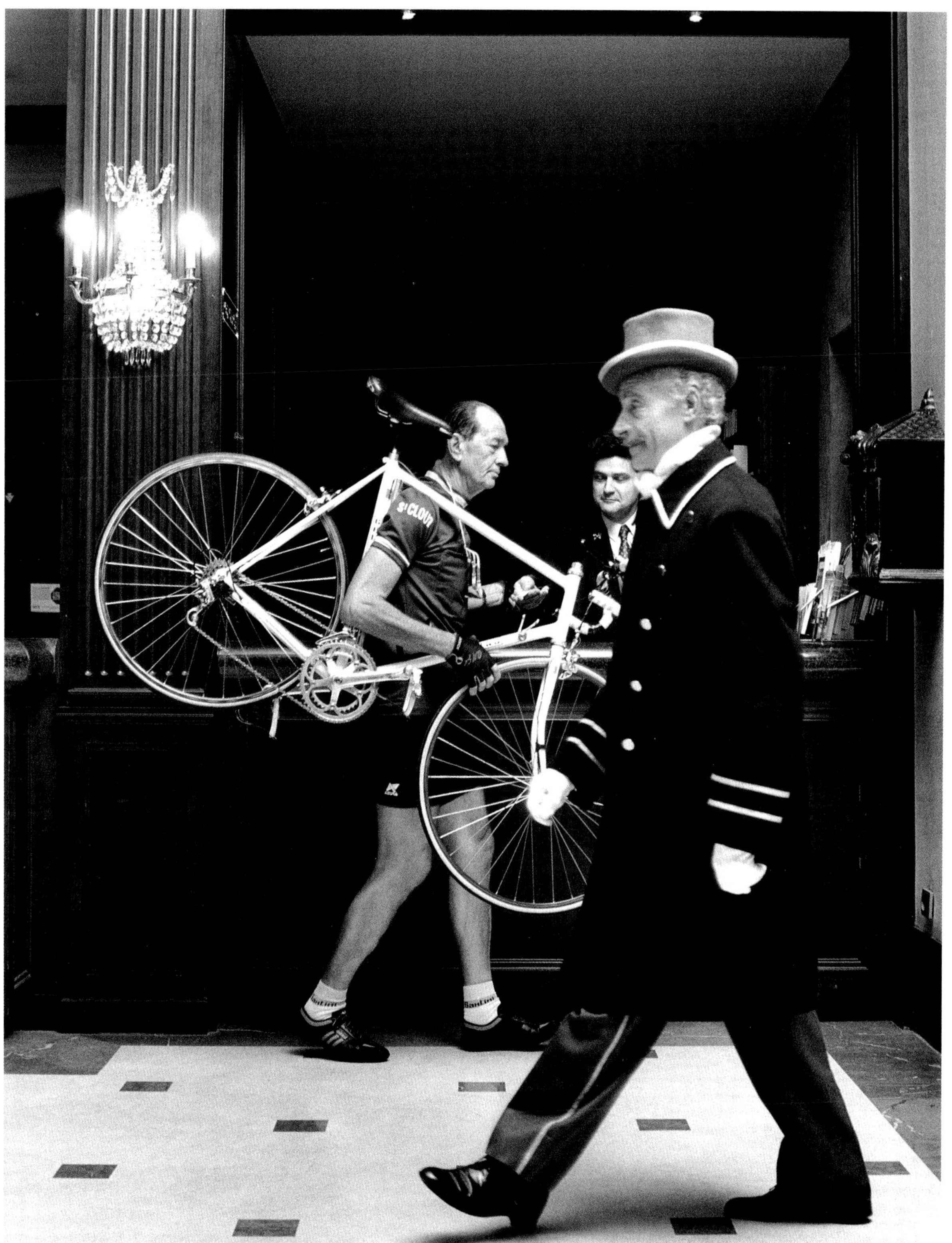

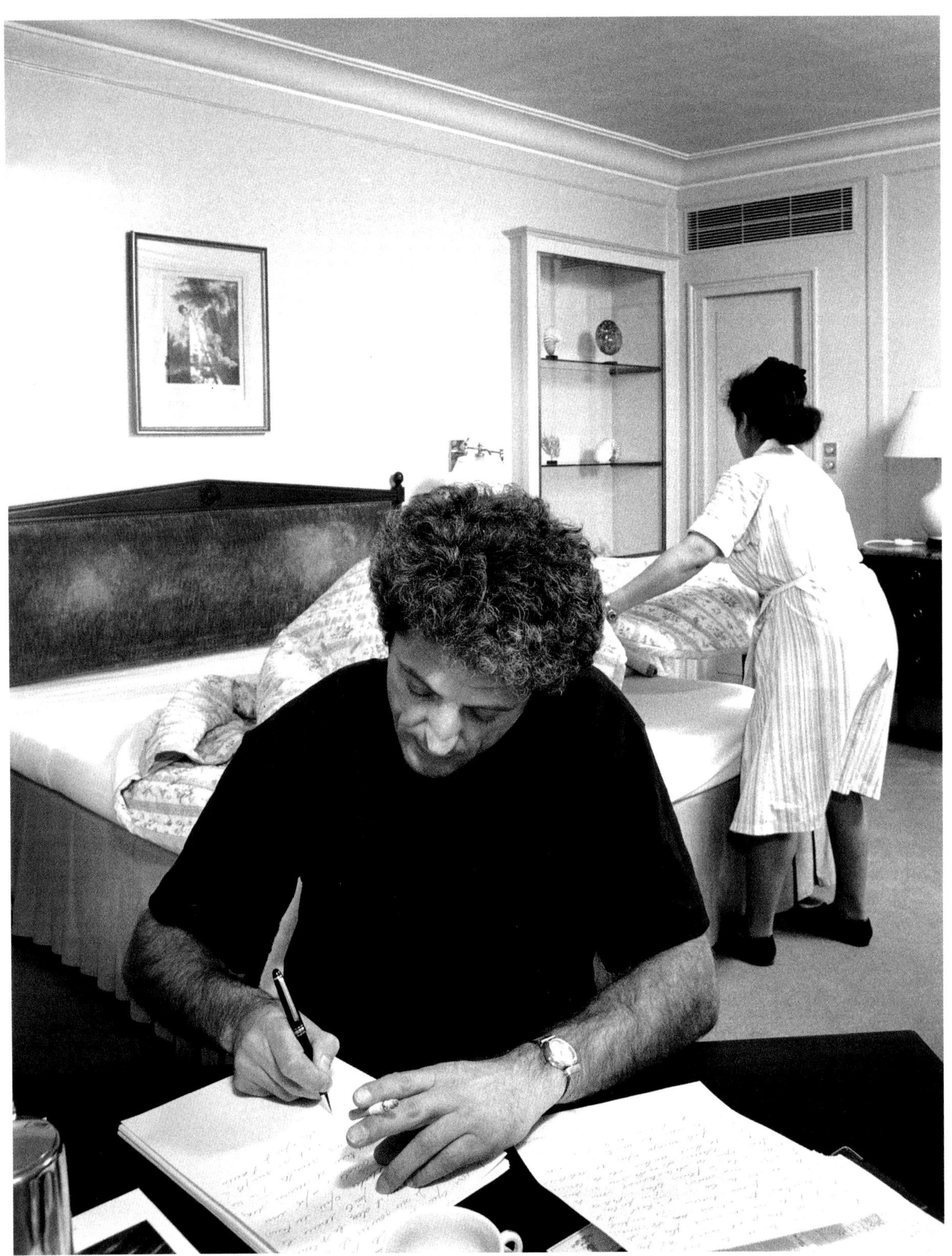

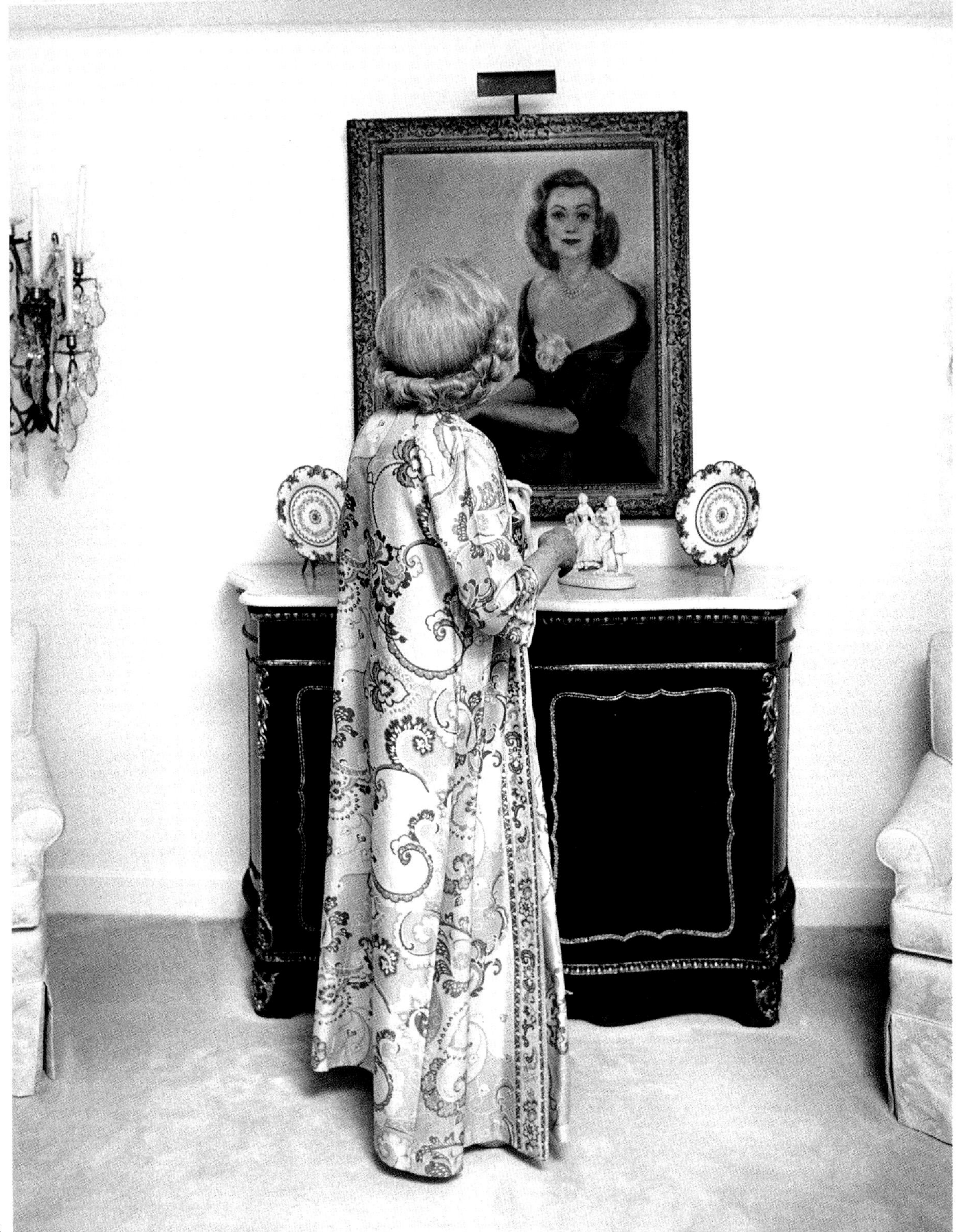

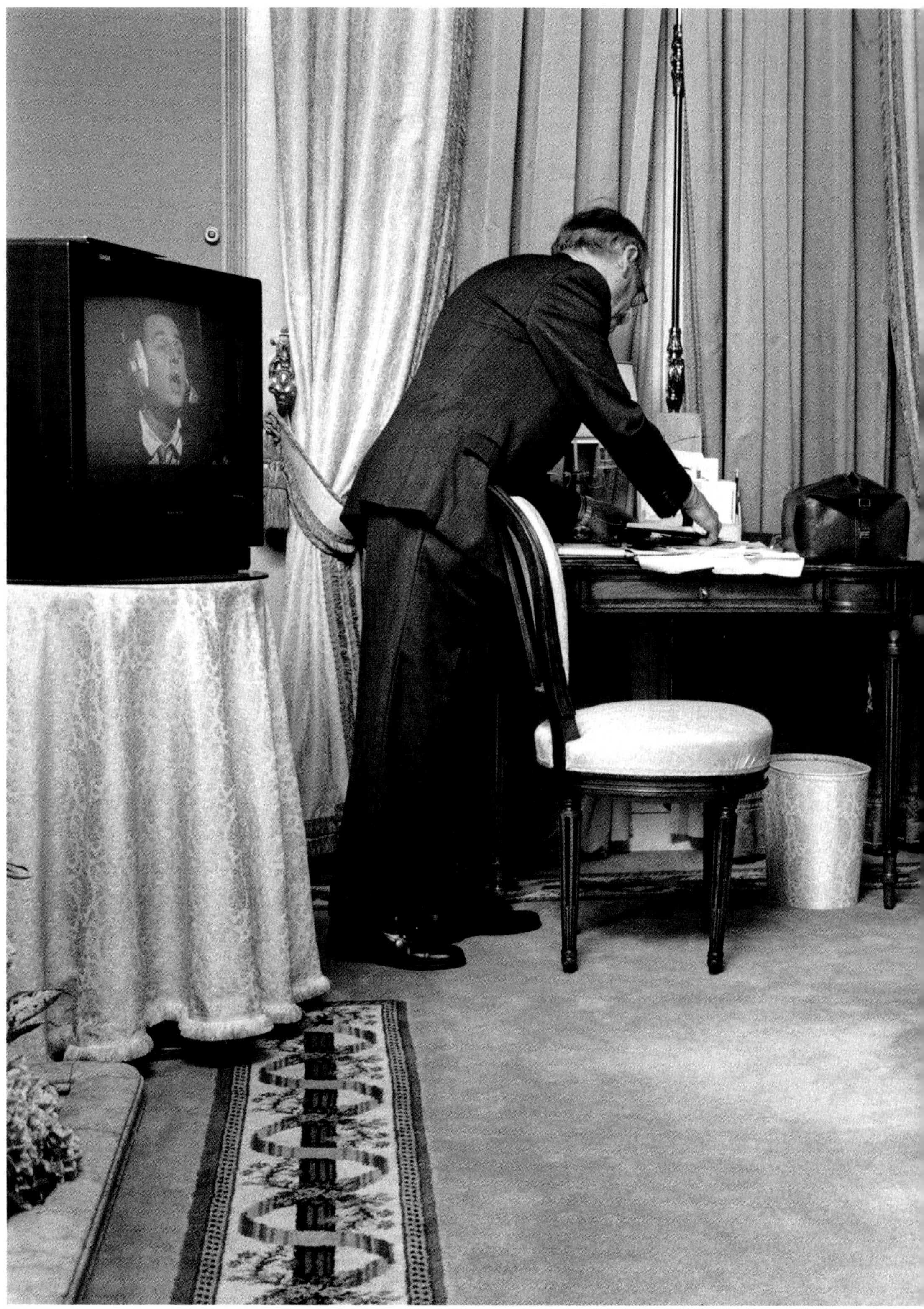

7

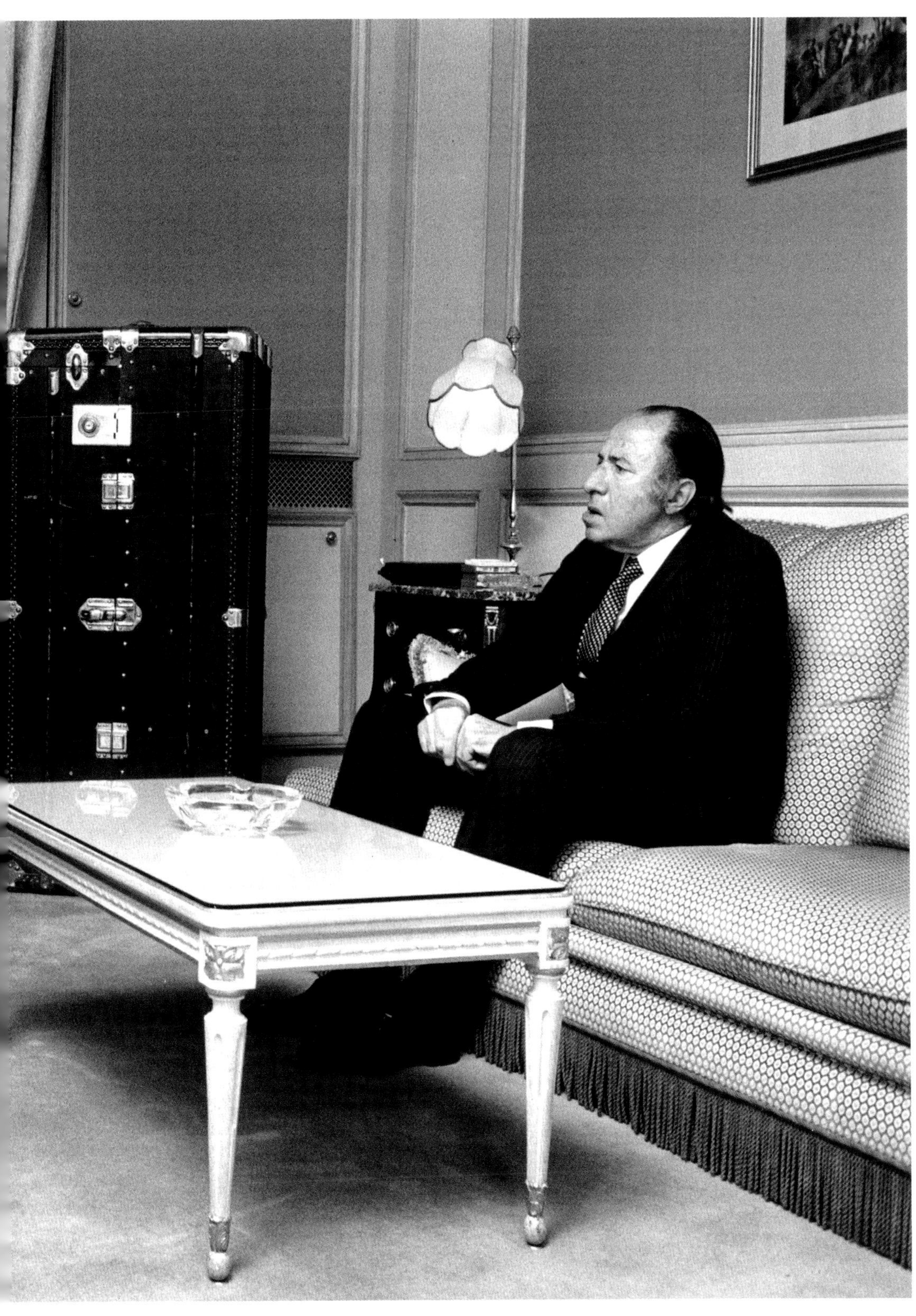

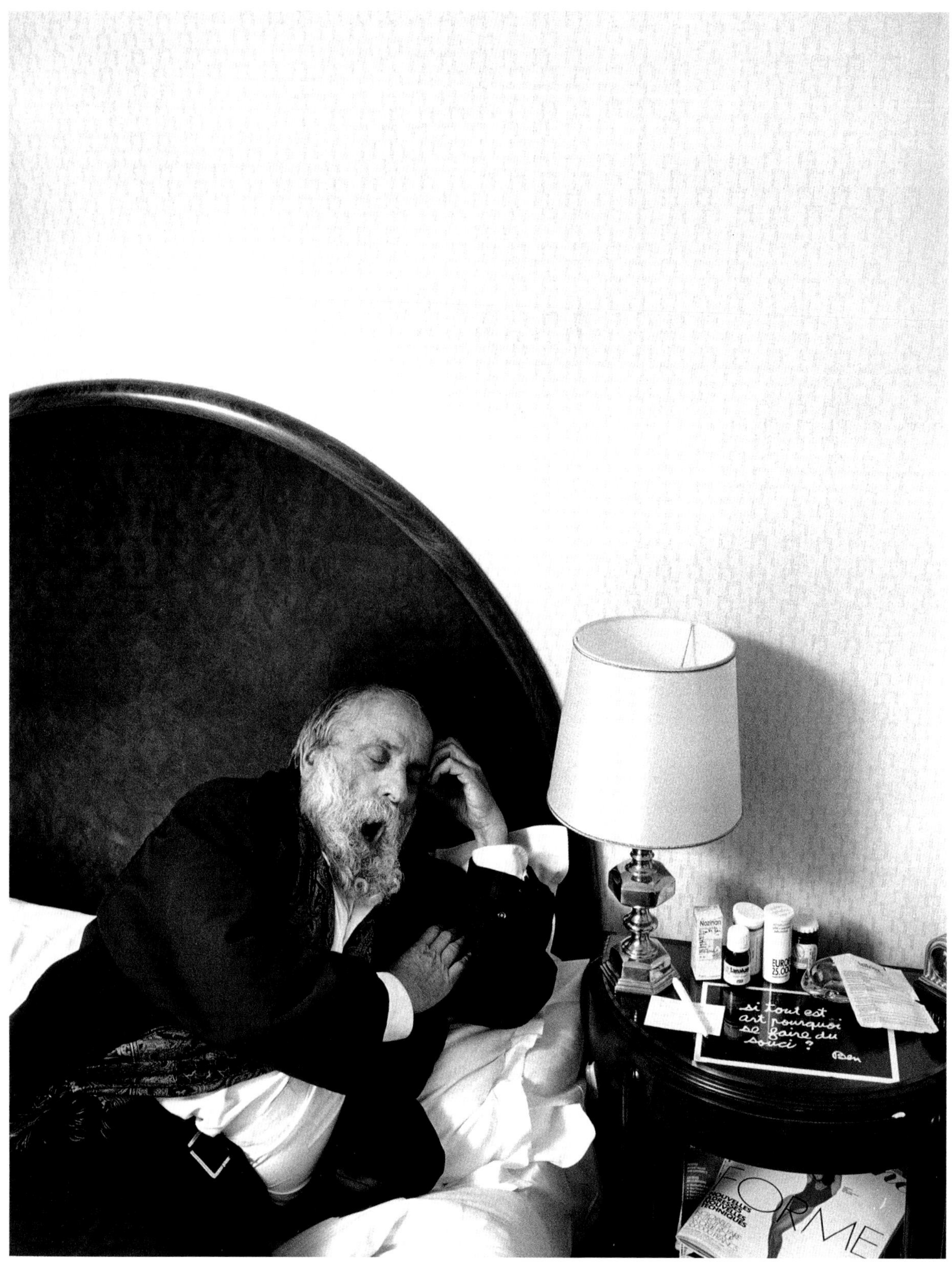
si tout est
art pourquoi
se faire du
souci ?
Ben
FORME

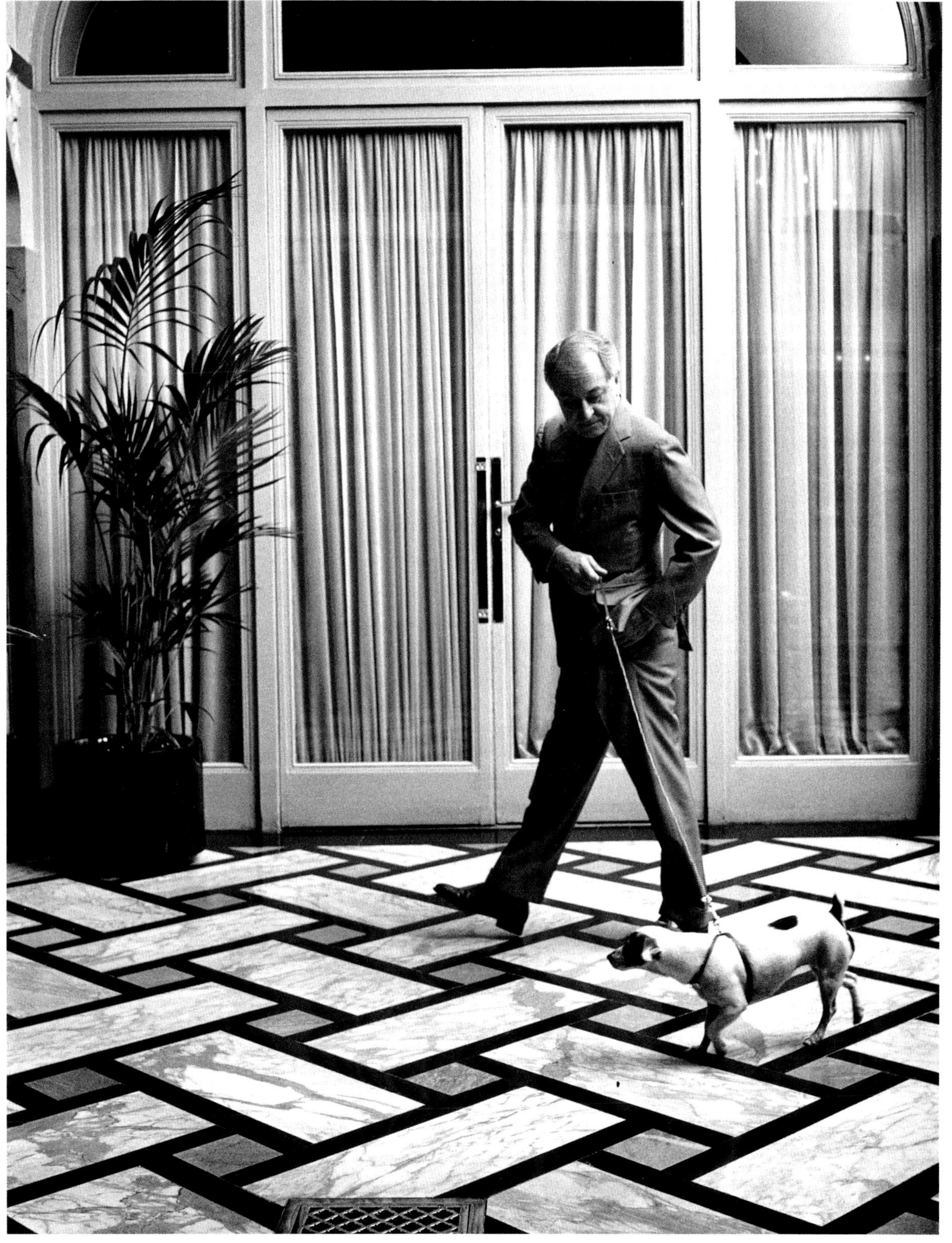

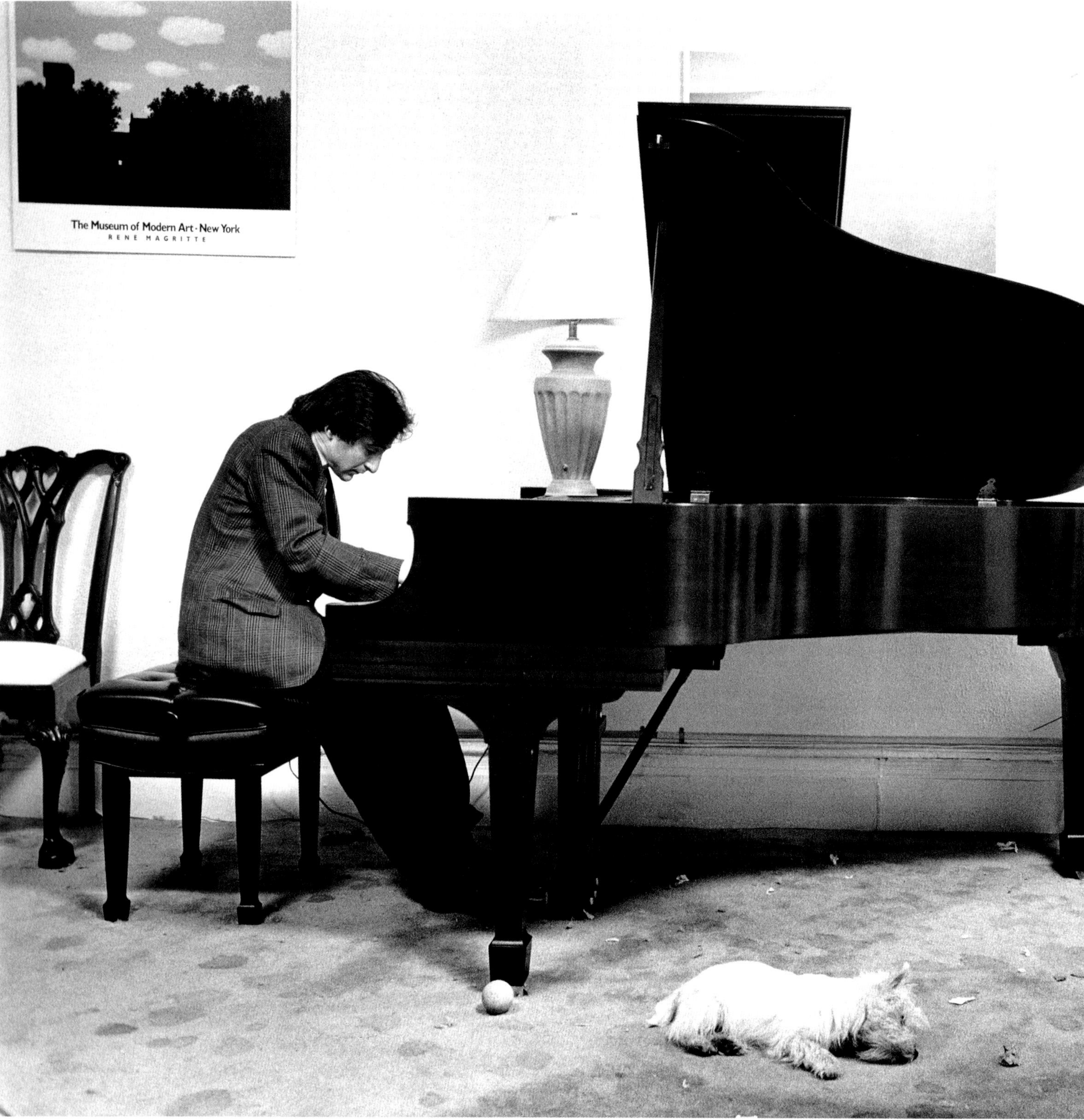
The Museum of Modern Art · New York
RENE MAGRITTE

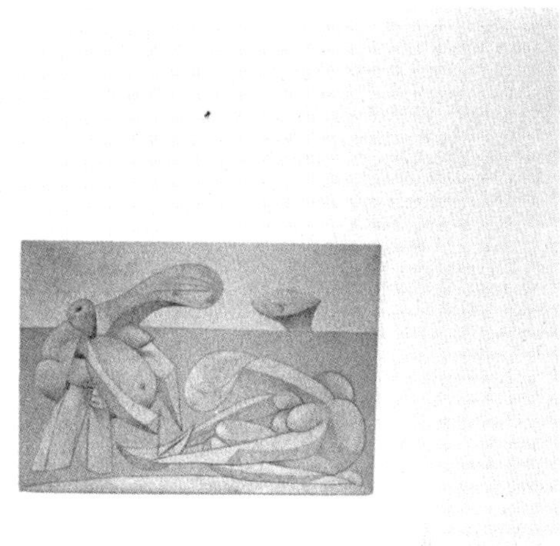

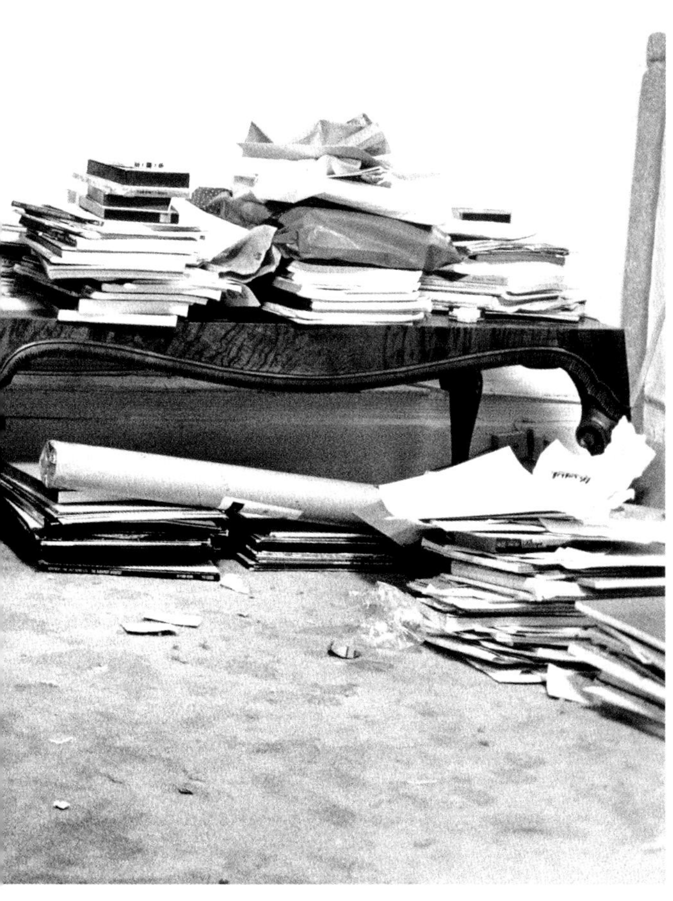

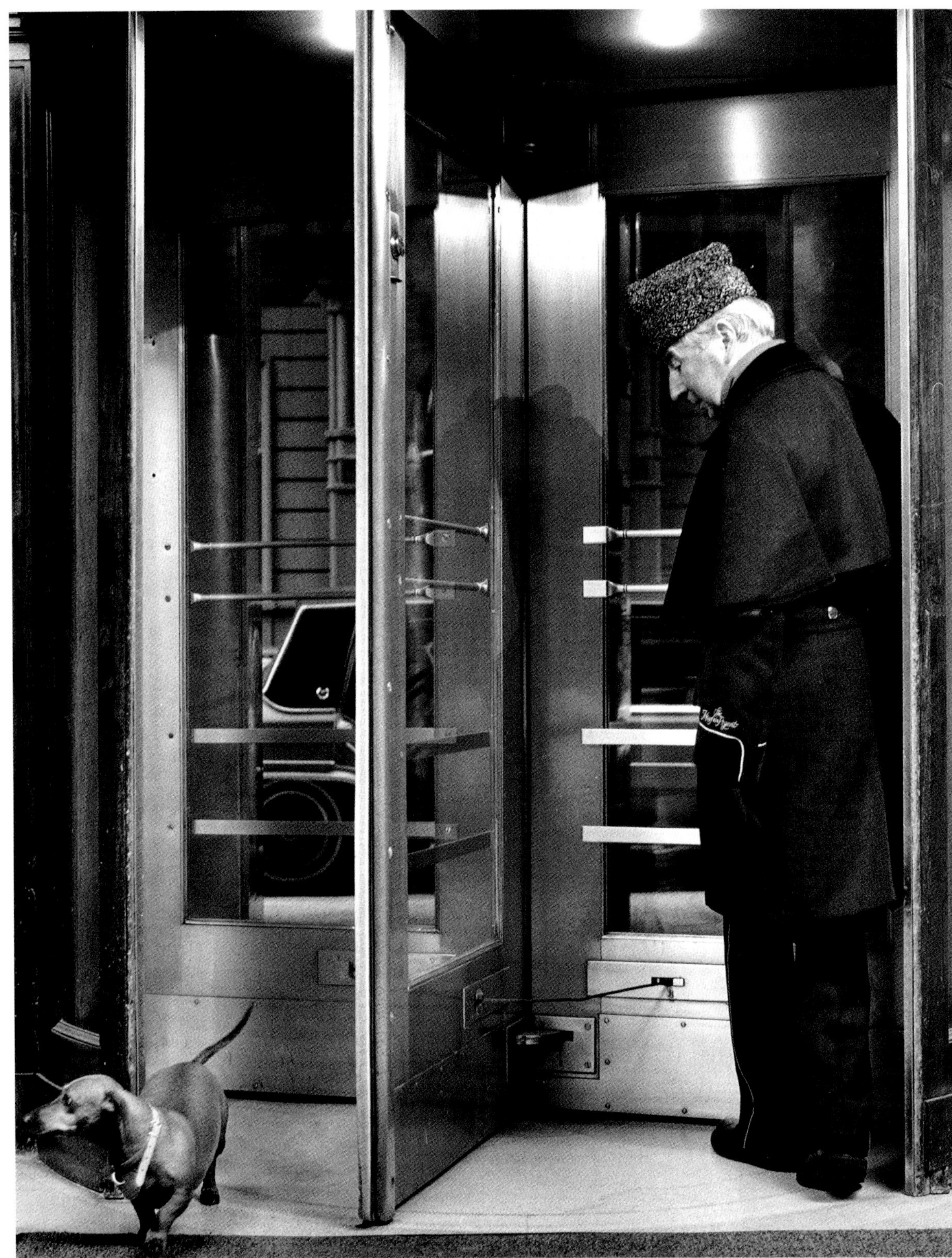

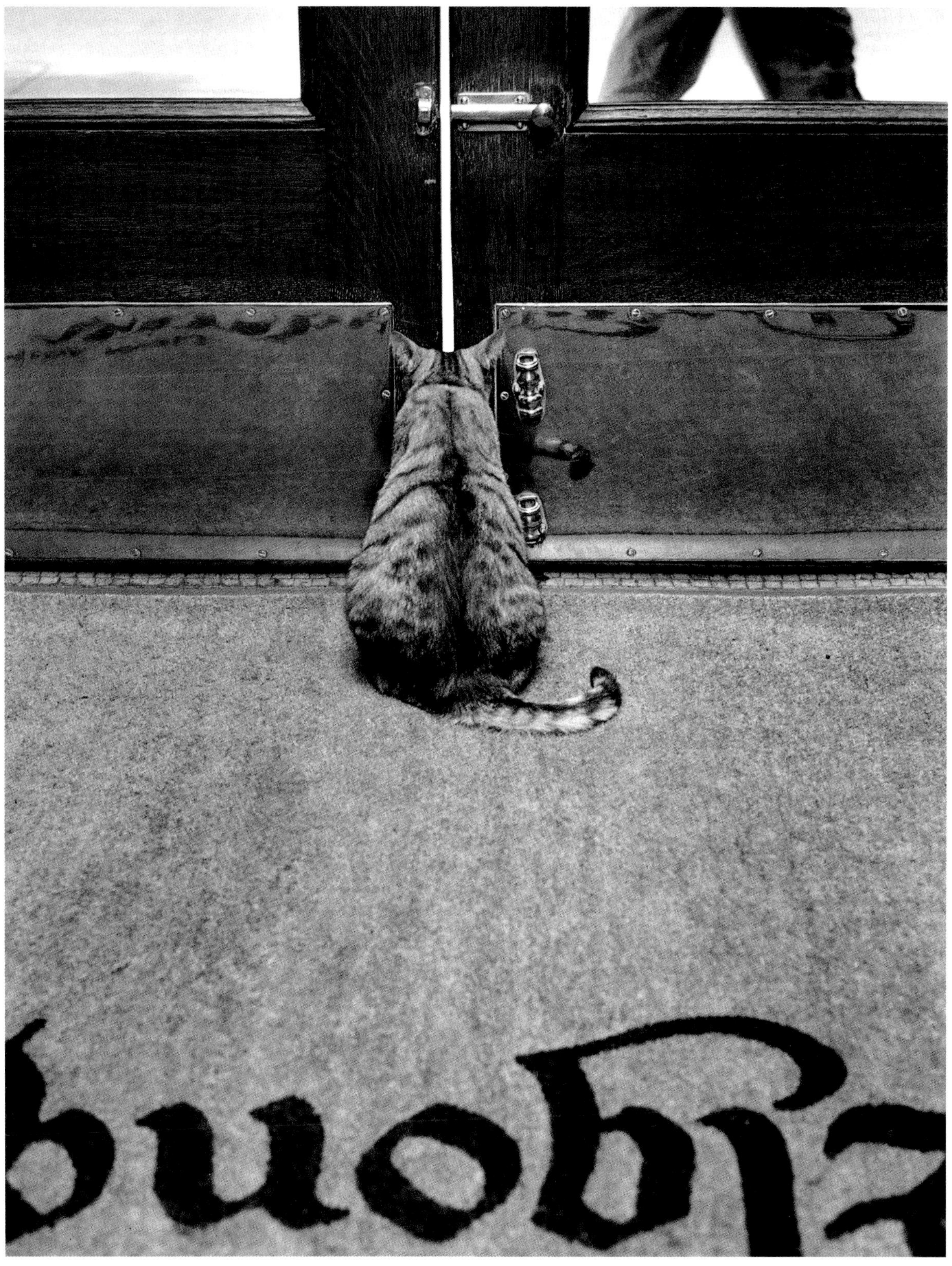

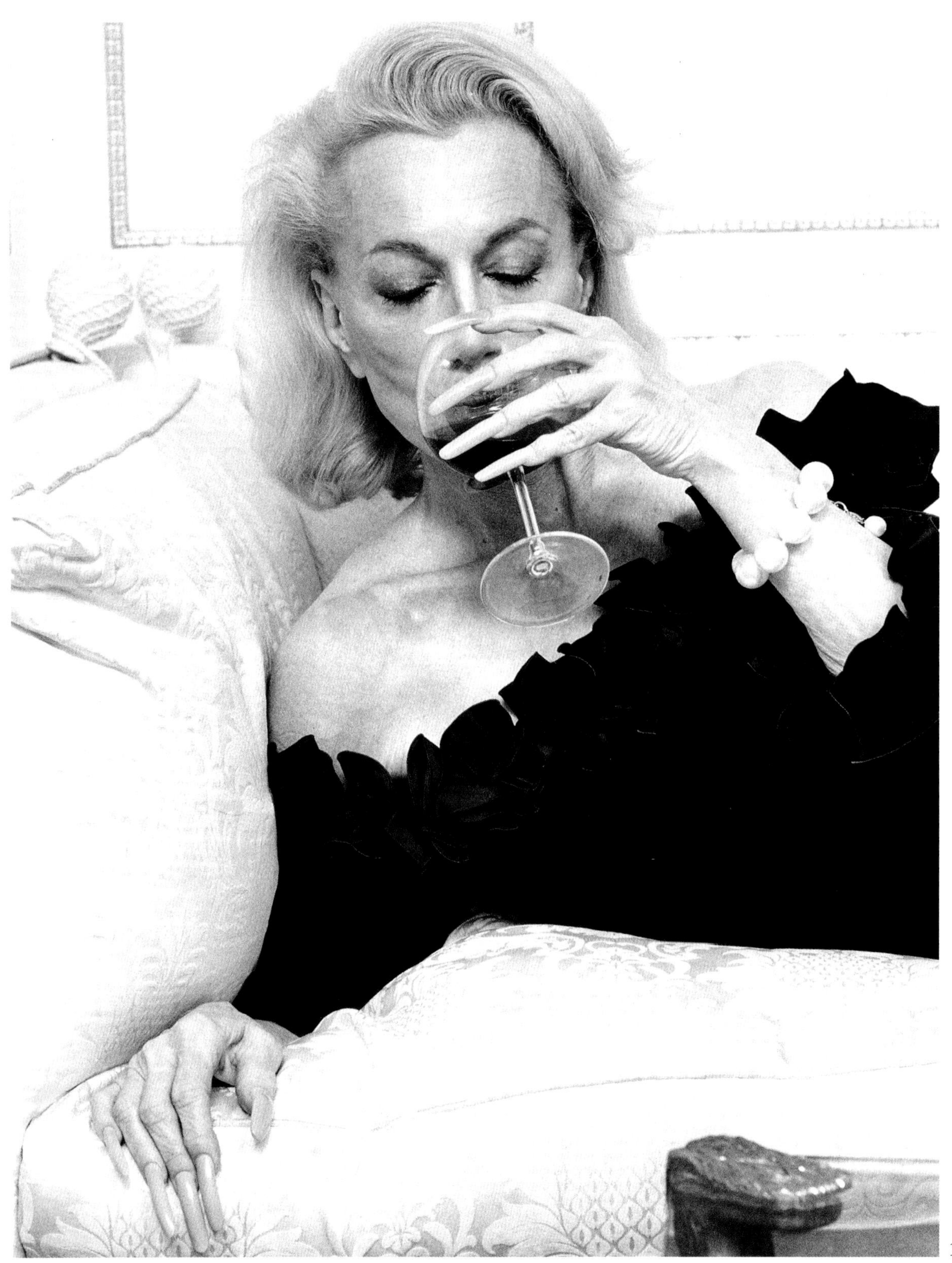

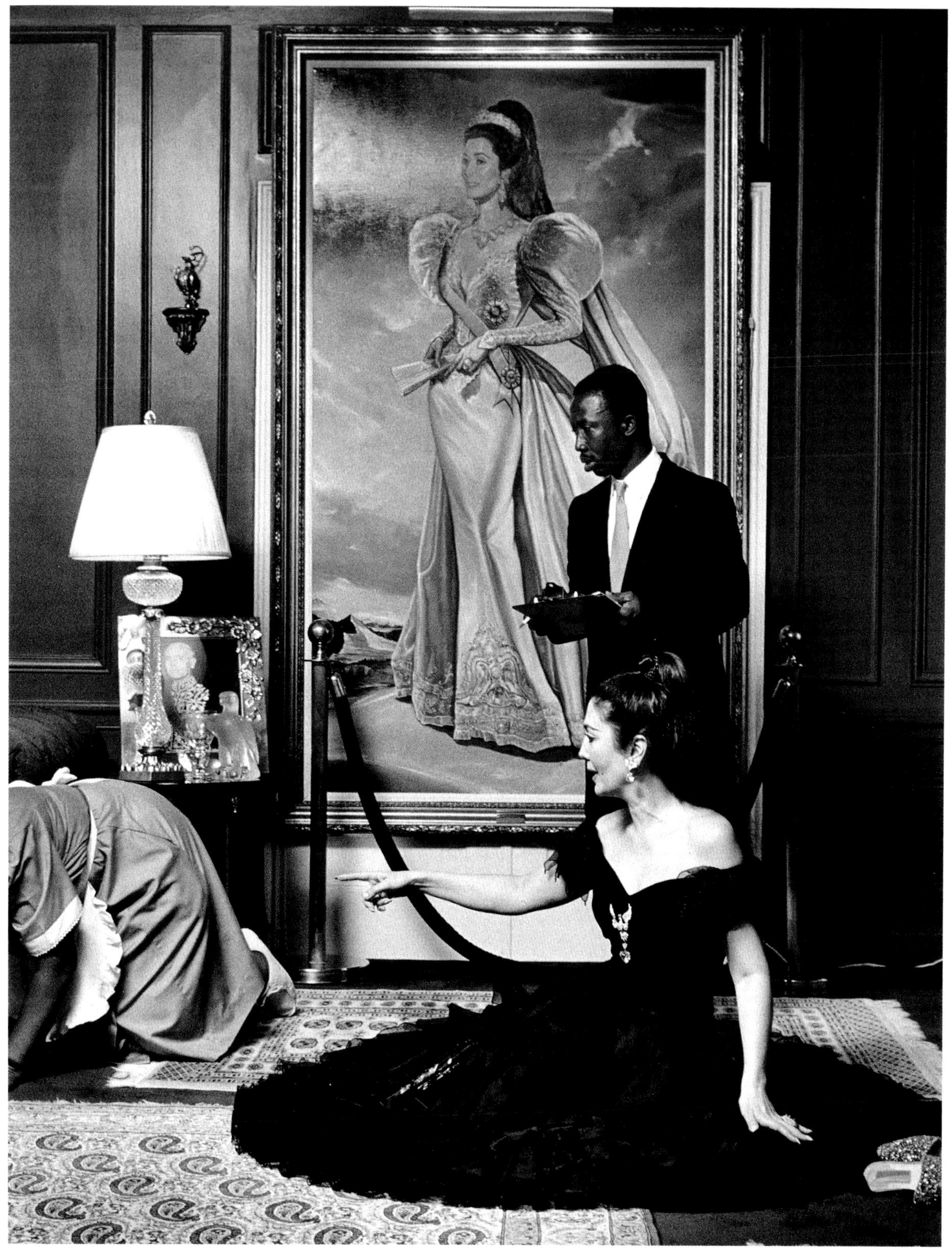

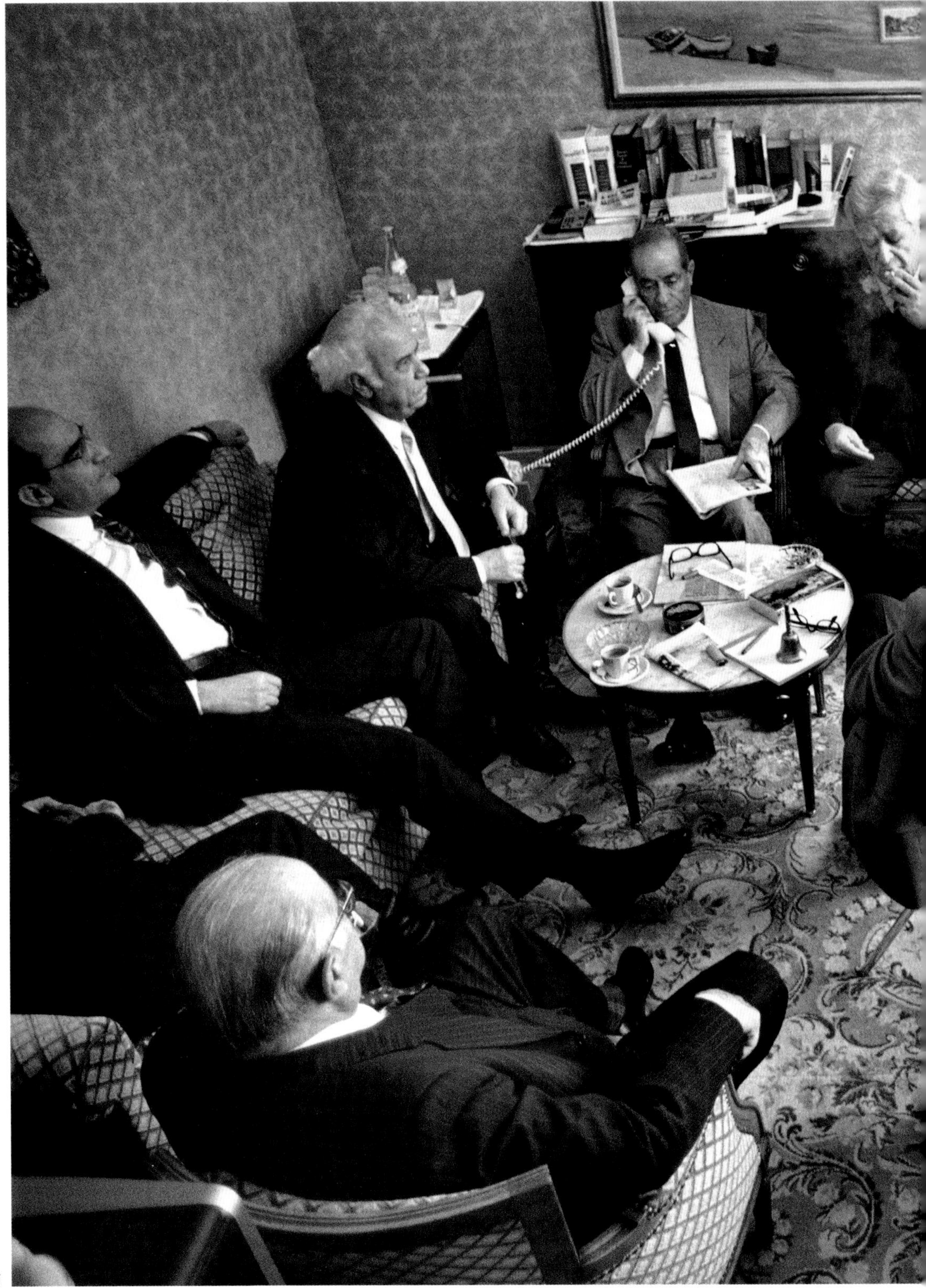

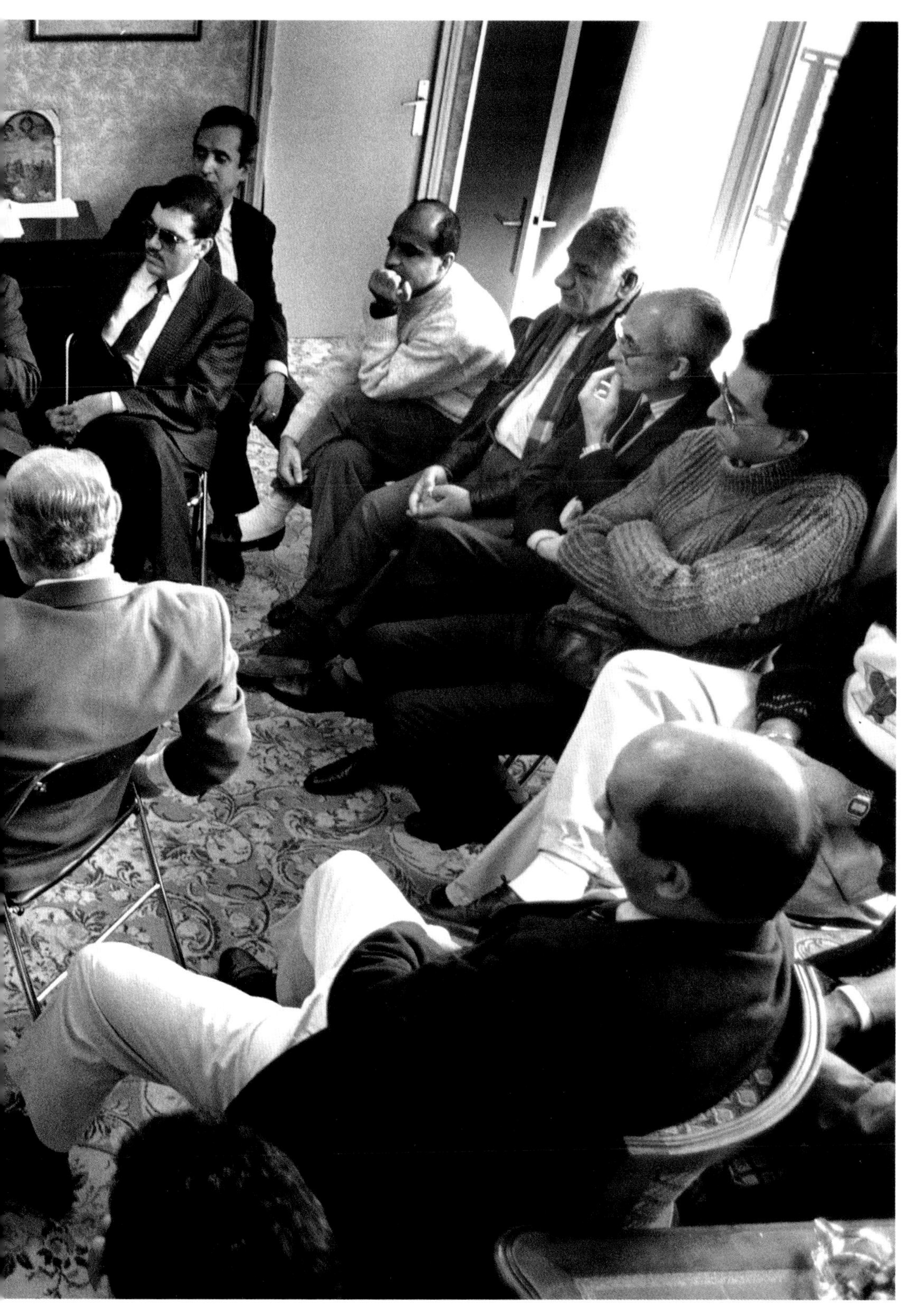

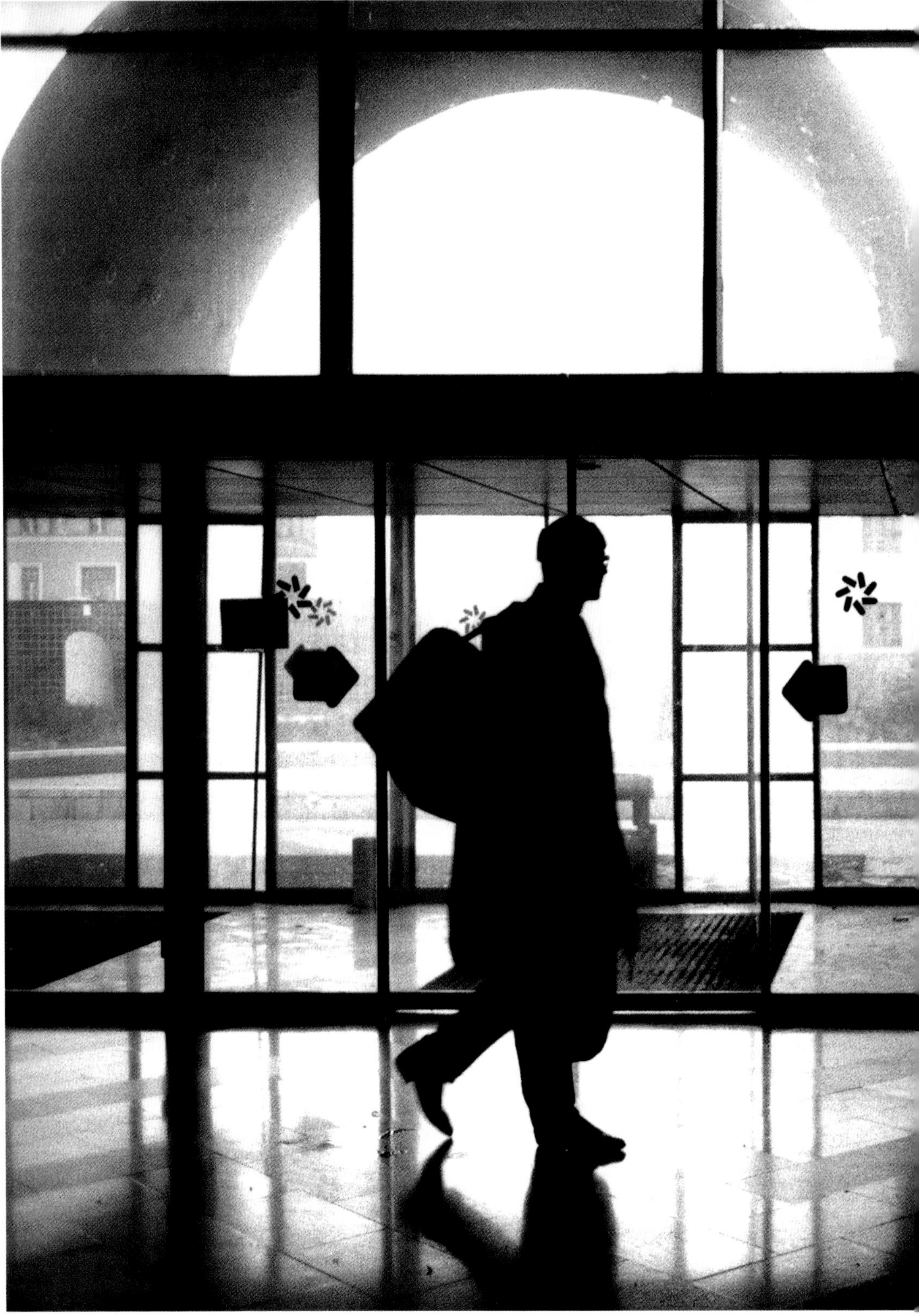

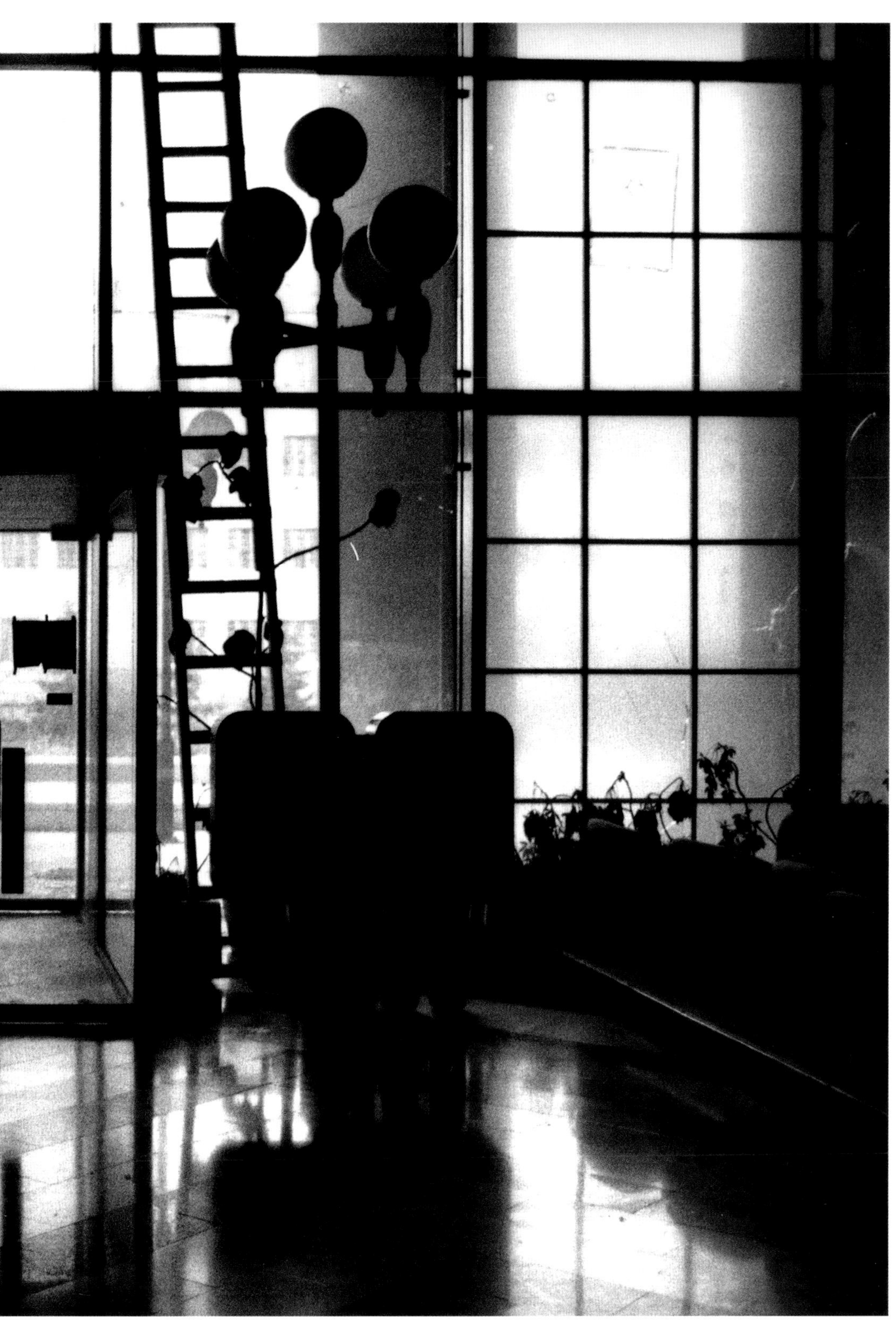

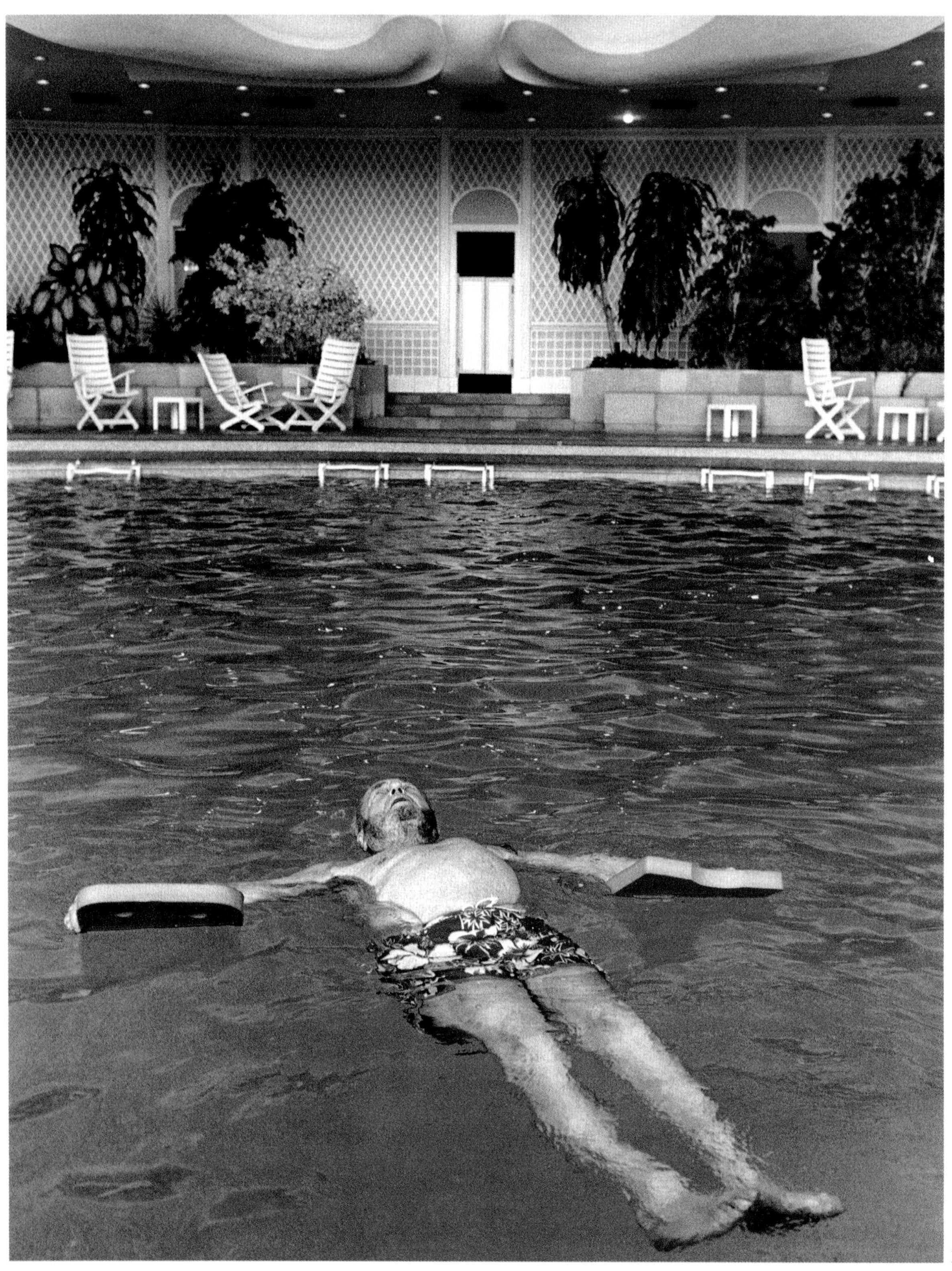

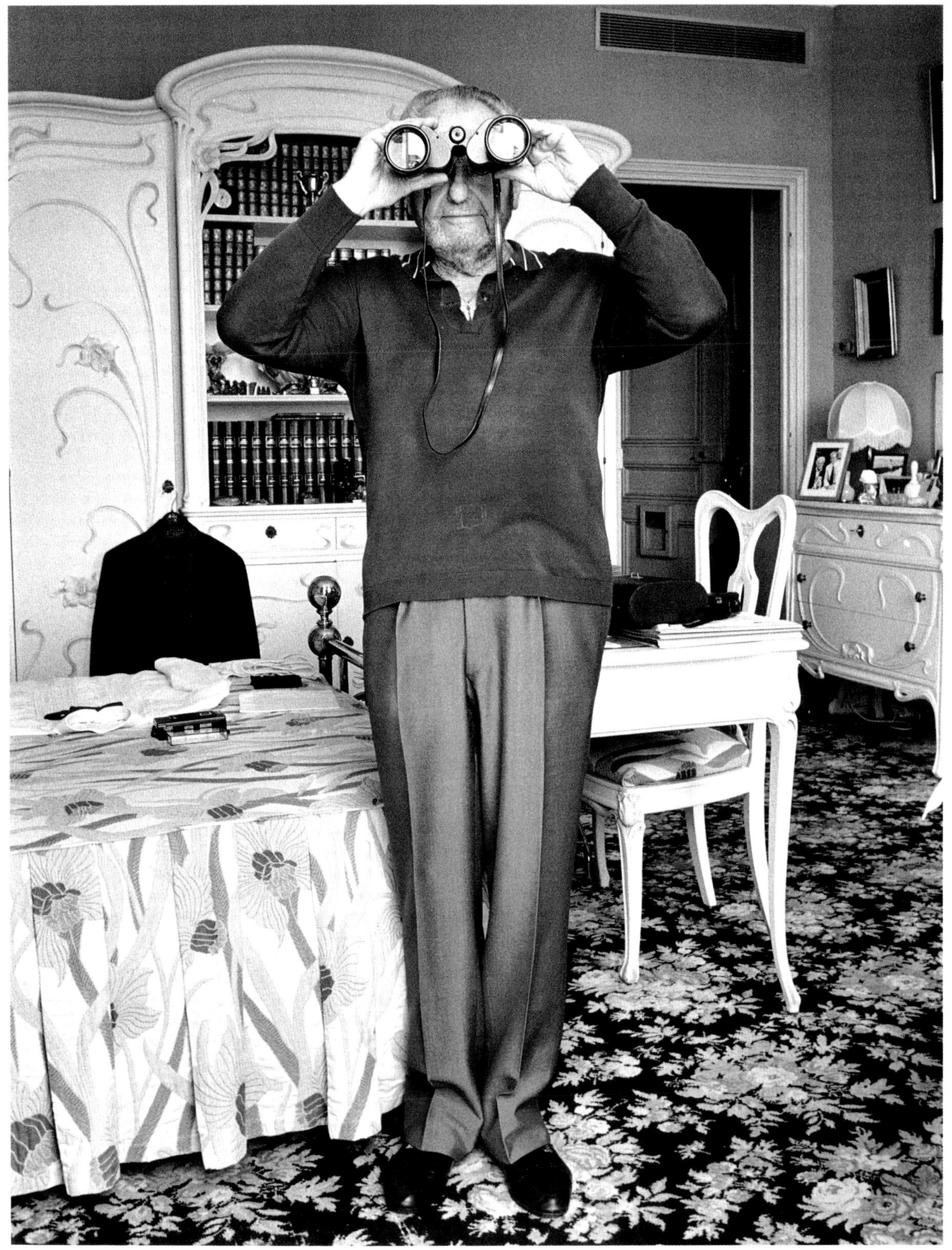

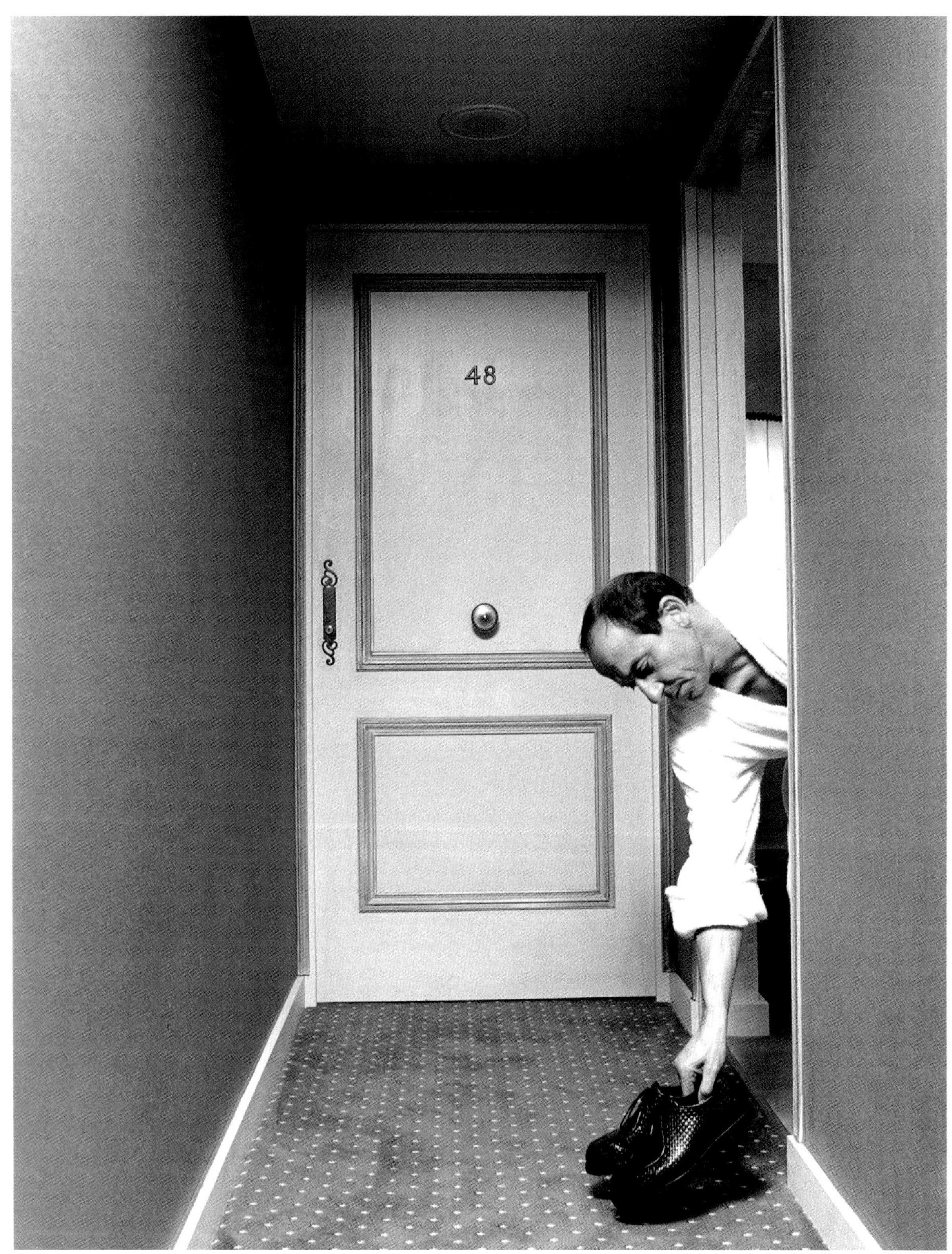
48

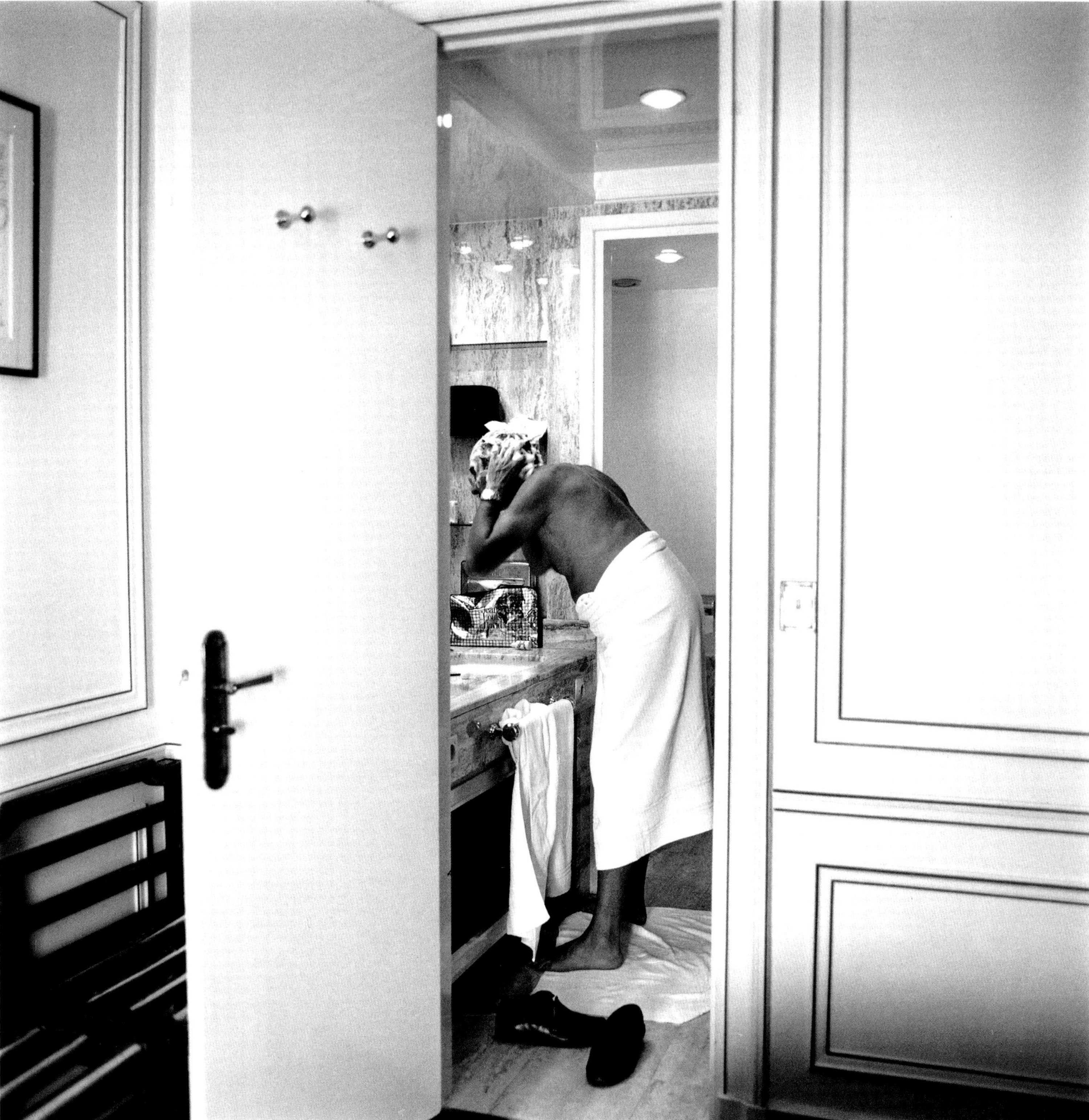

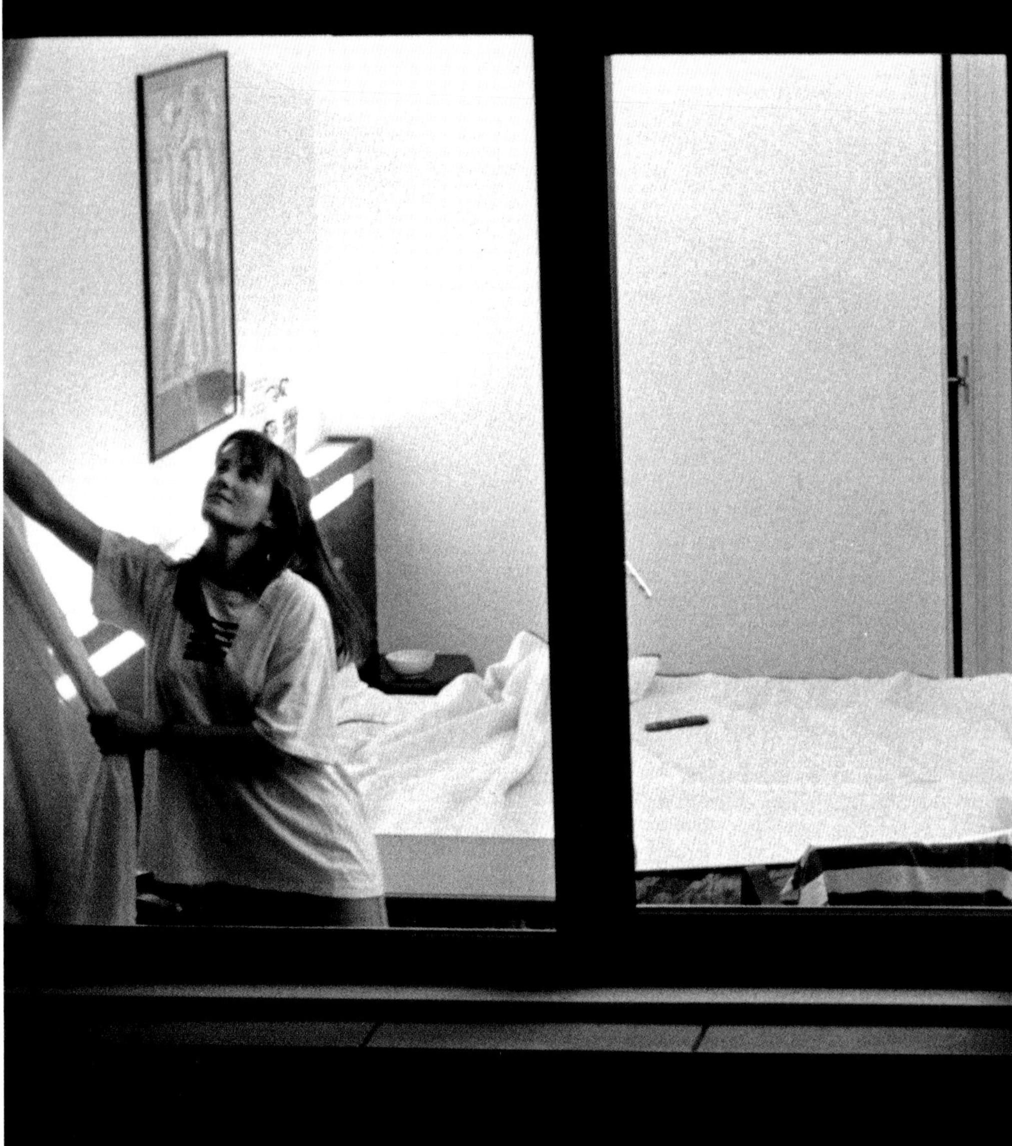

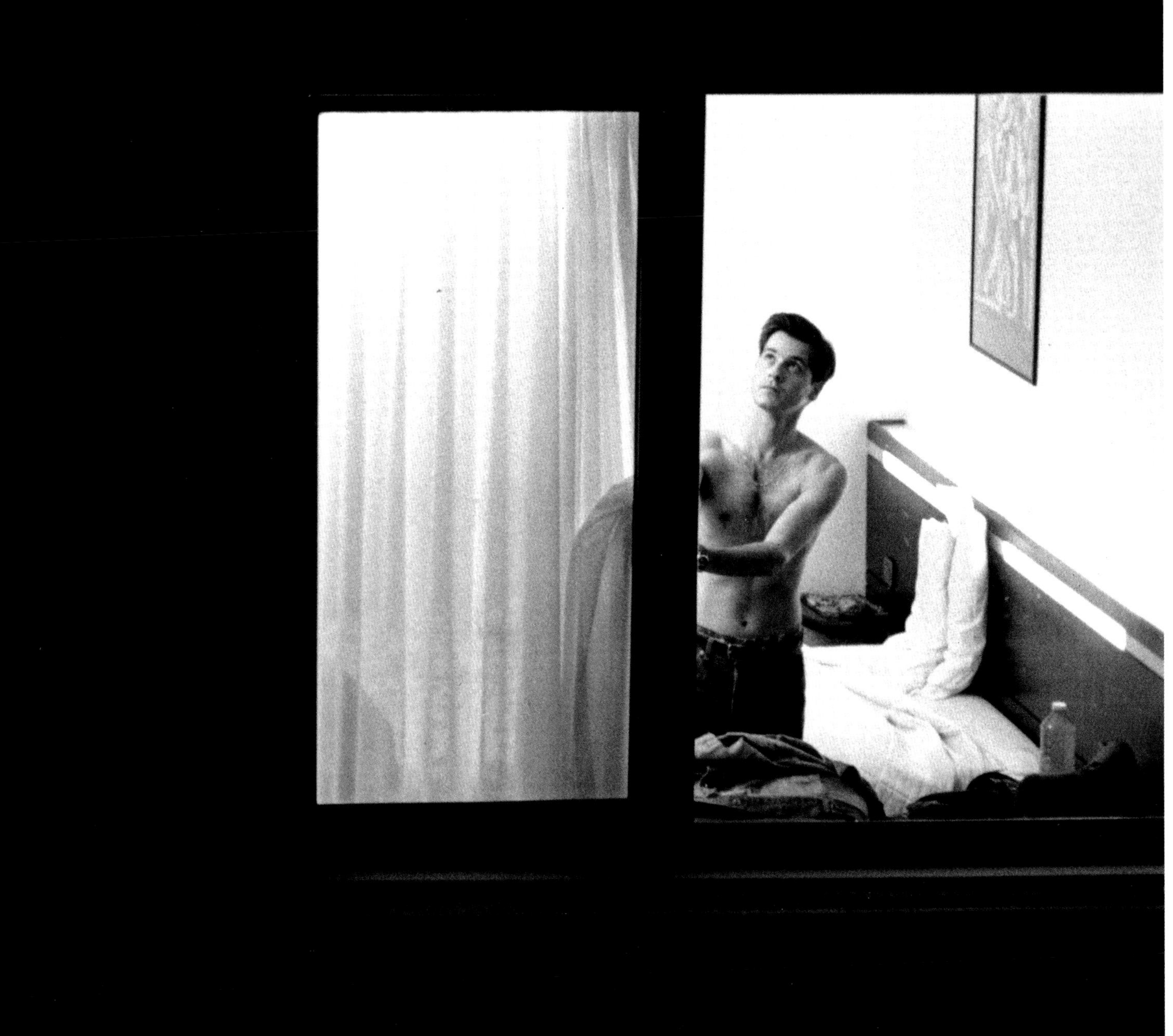

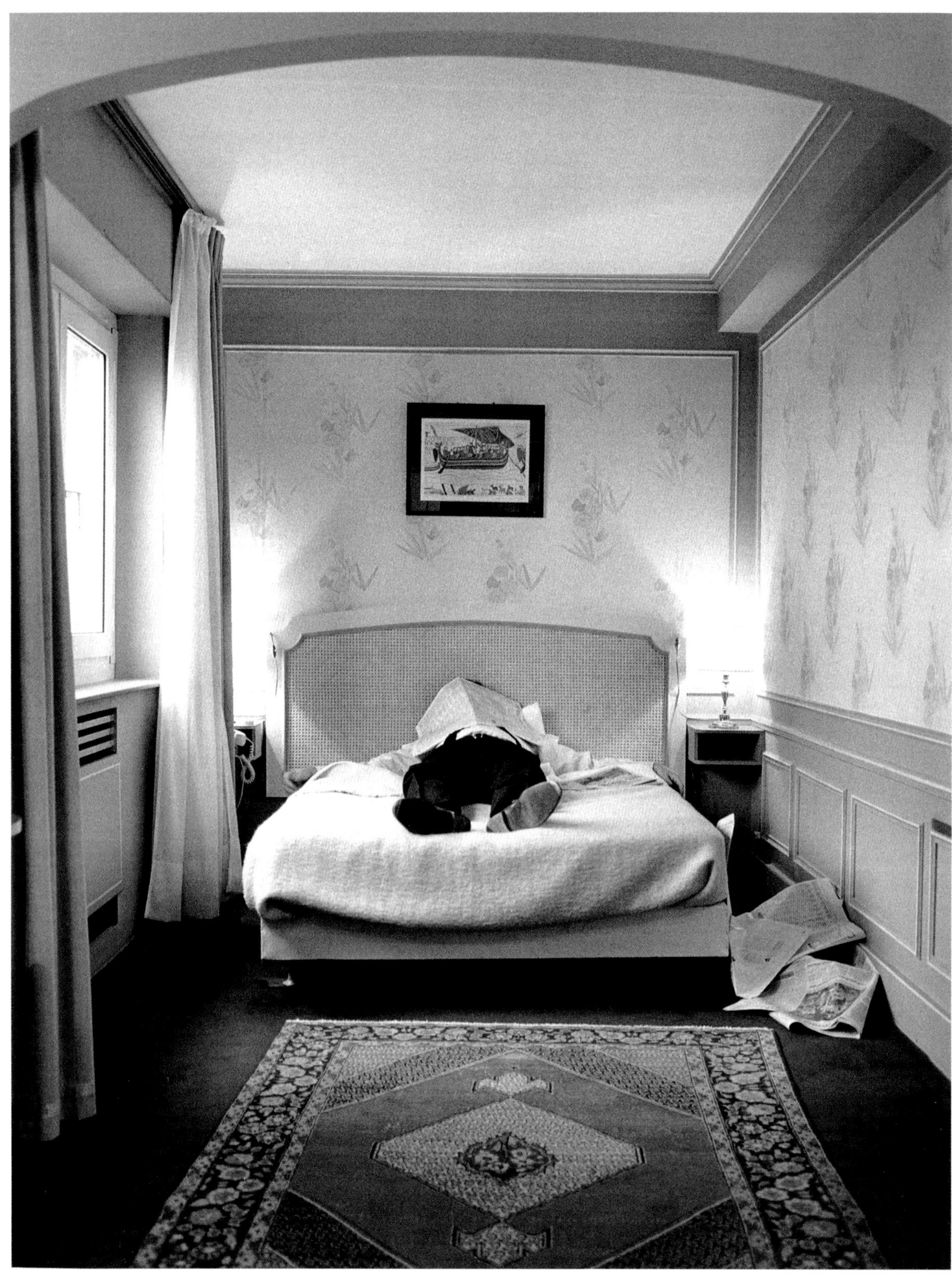

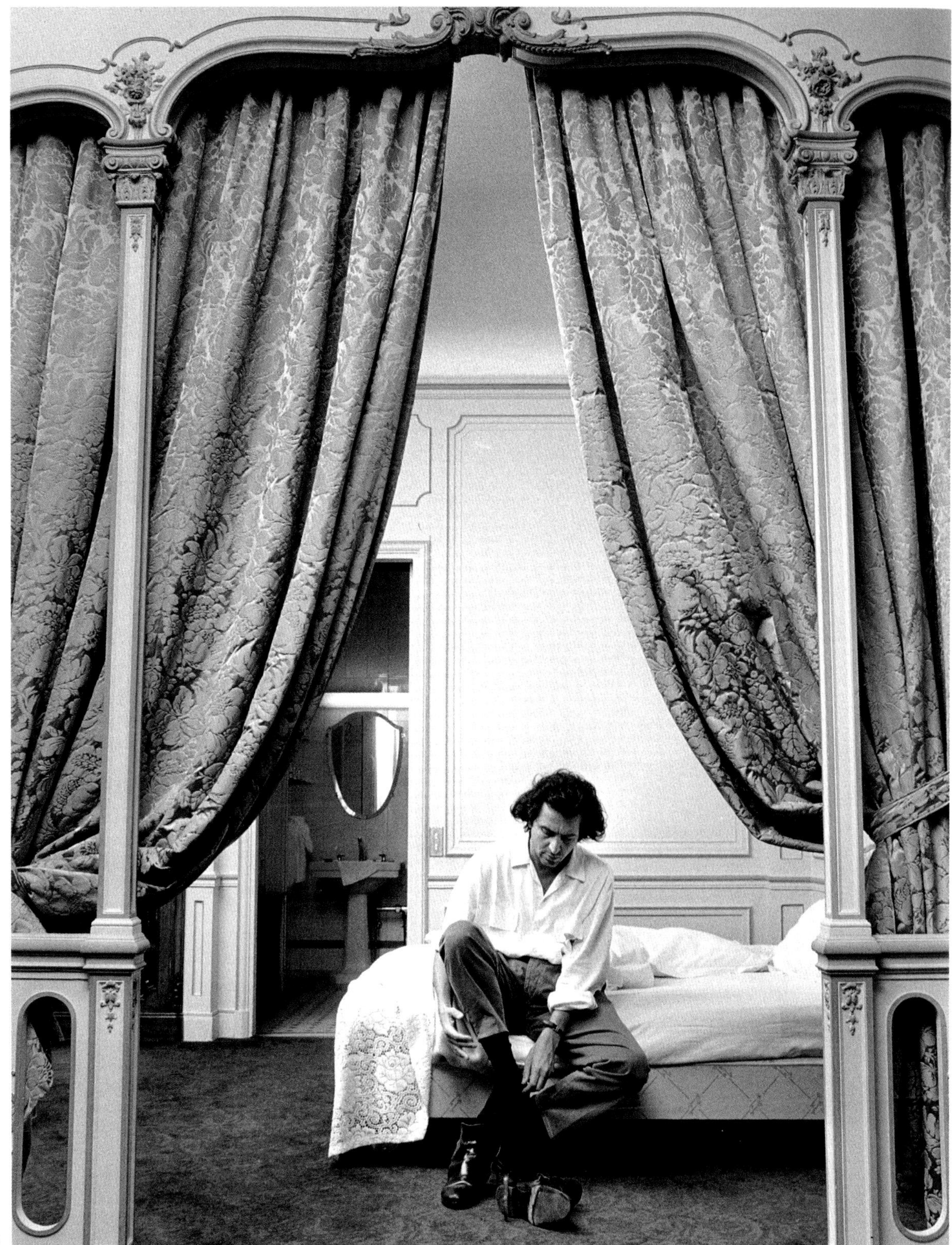

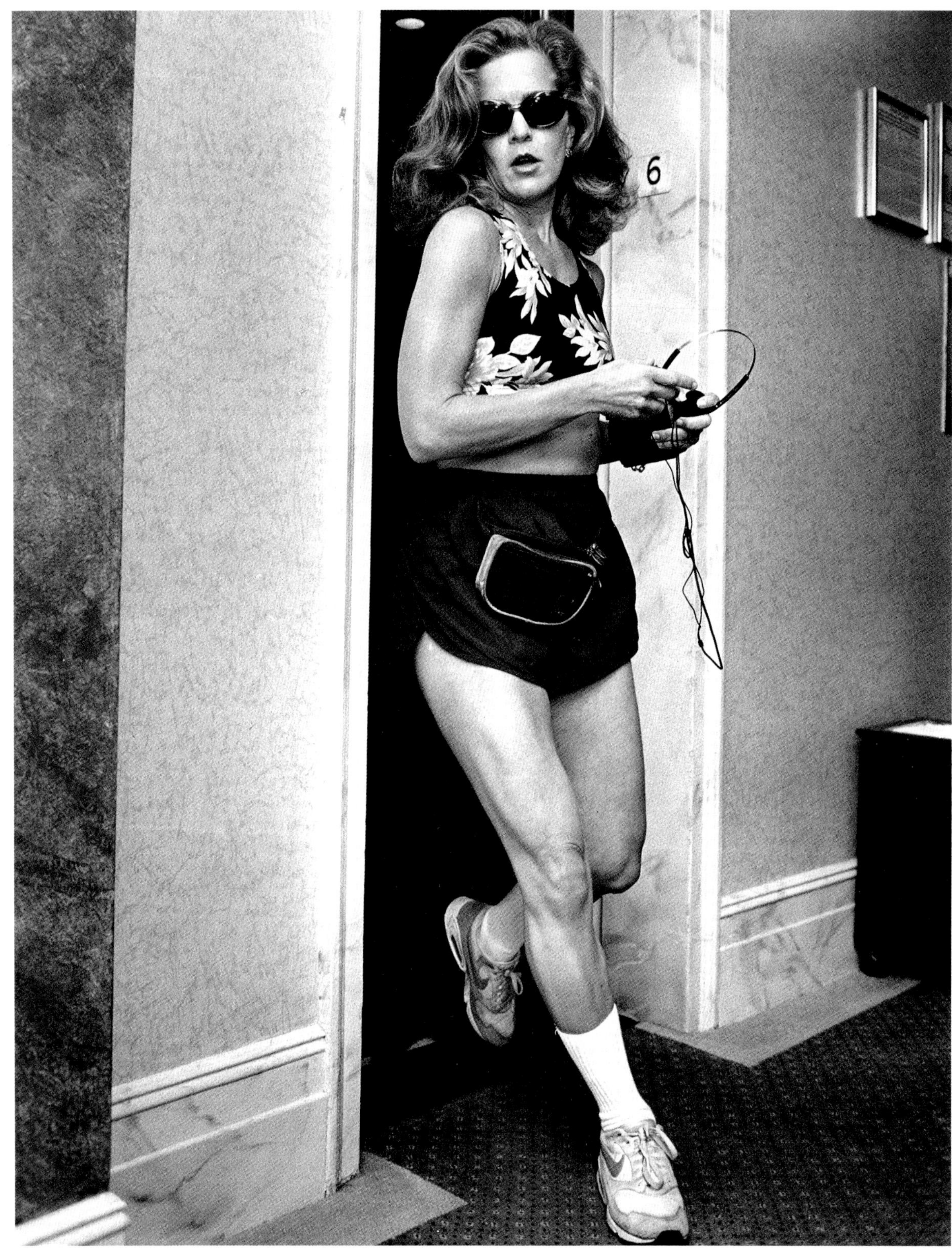
6

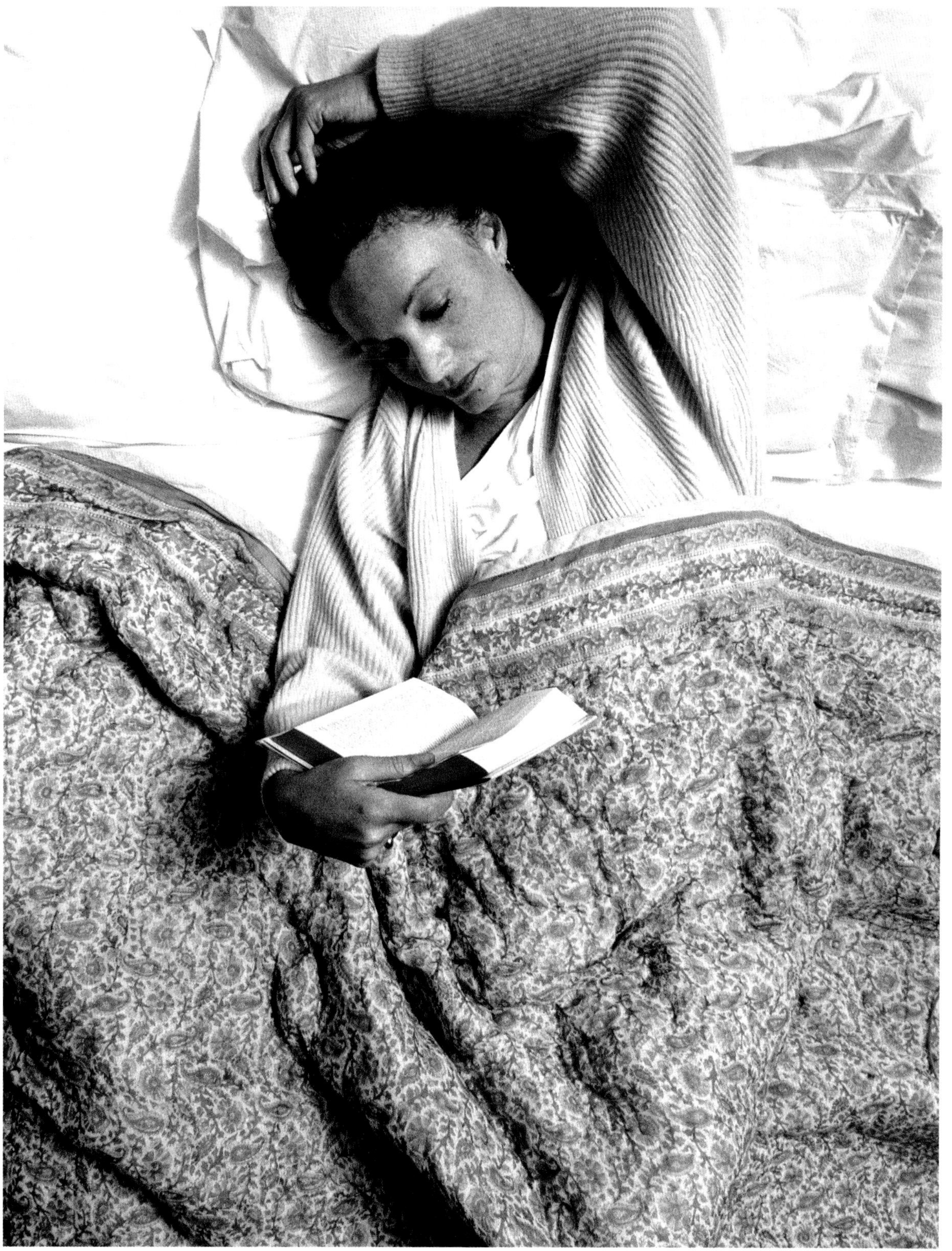

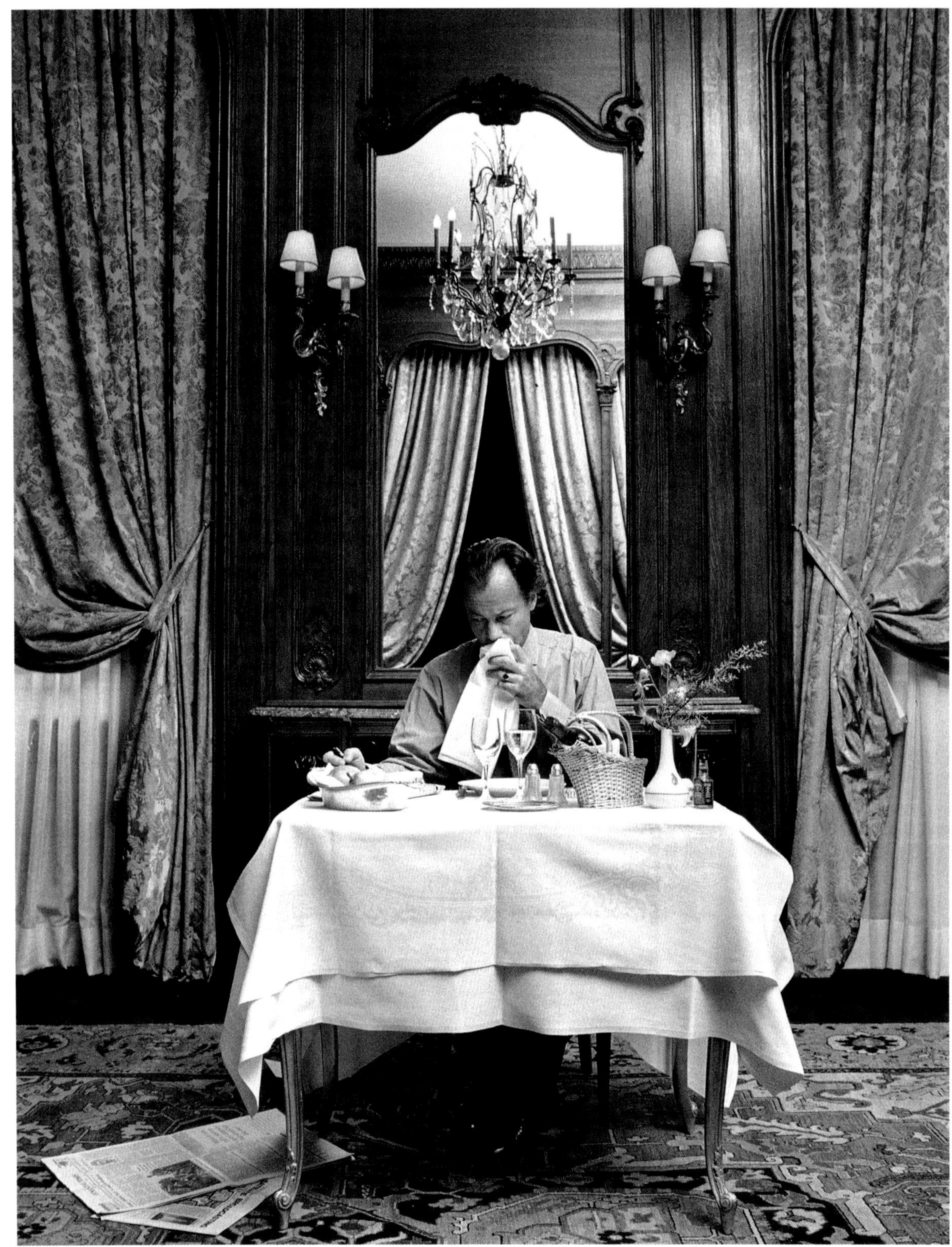

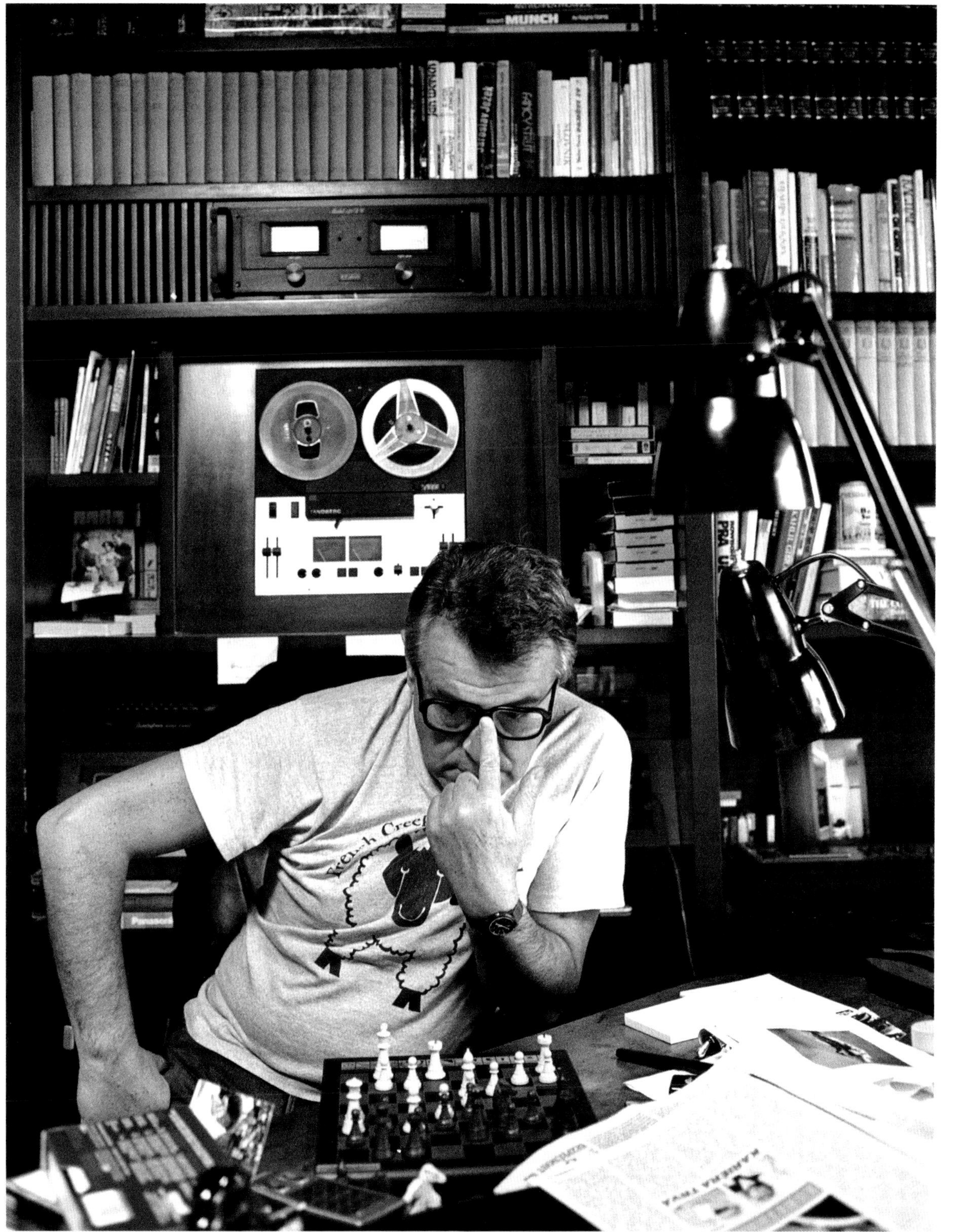
MUNCH

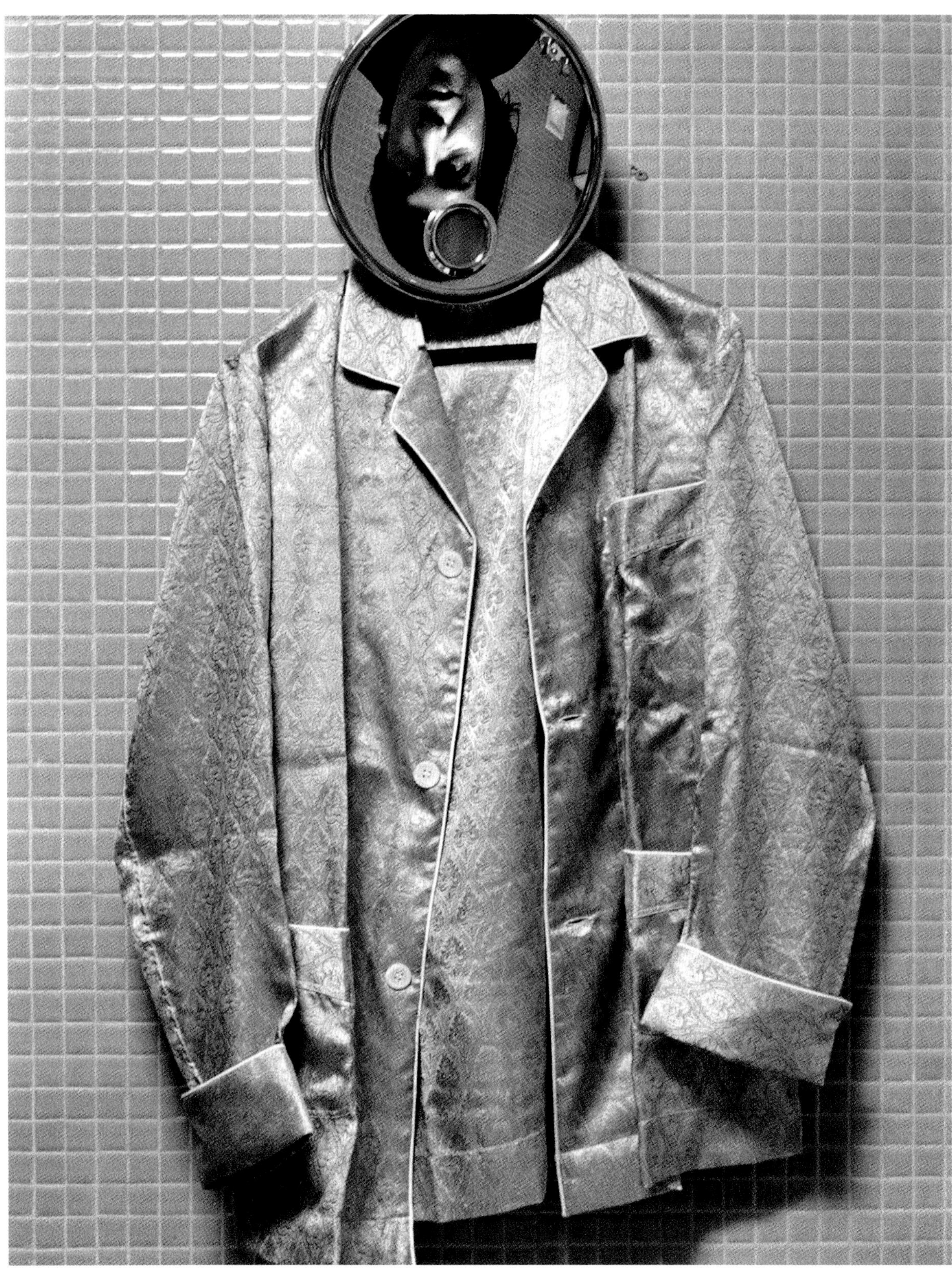

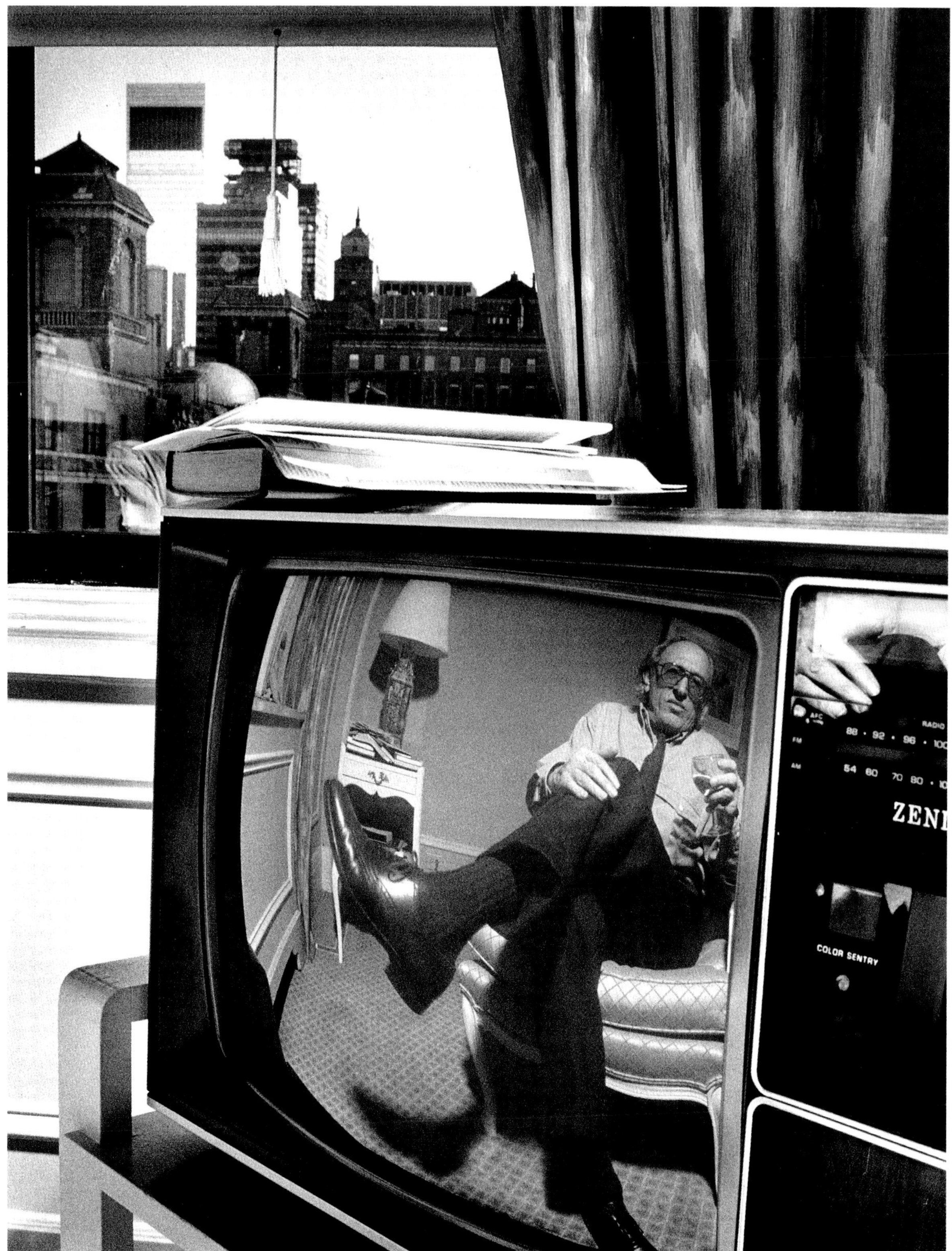
RADIO
FM
AM
COLOR SENTRY

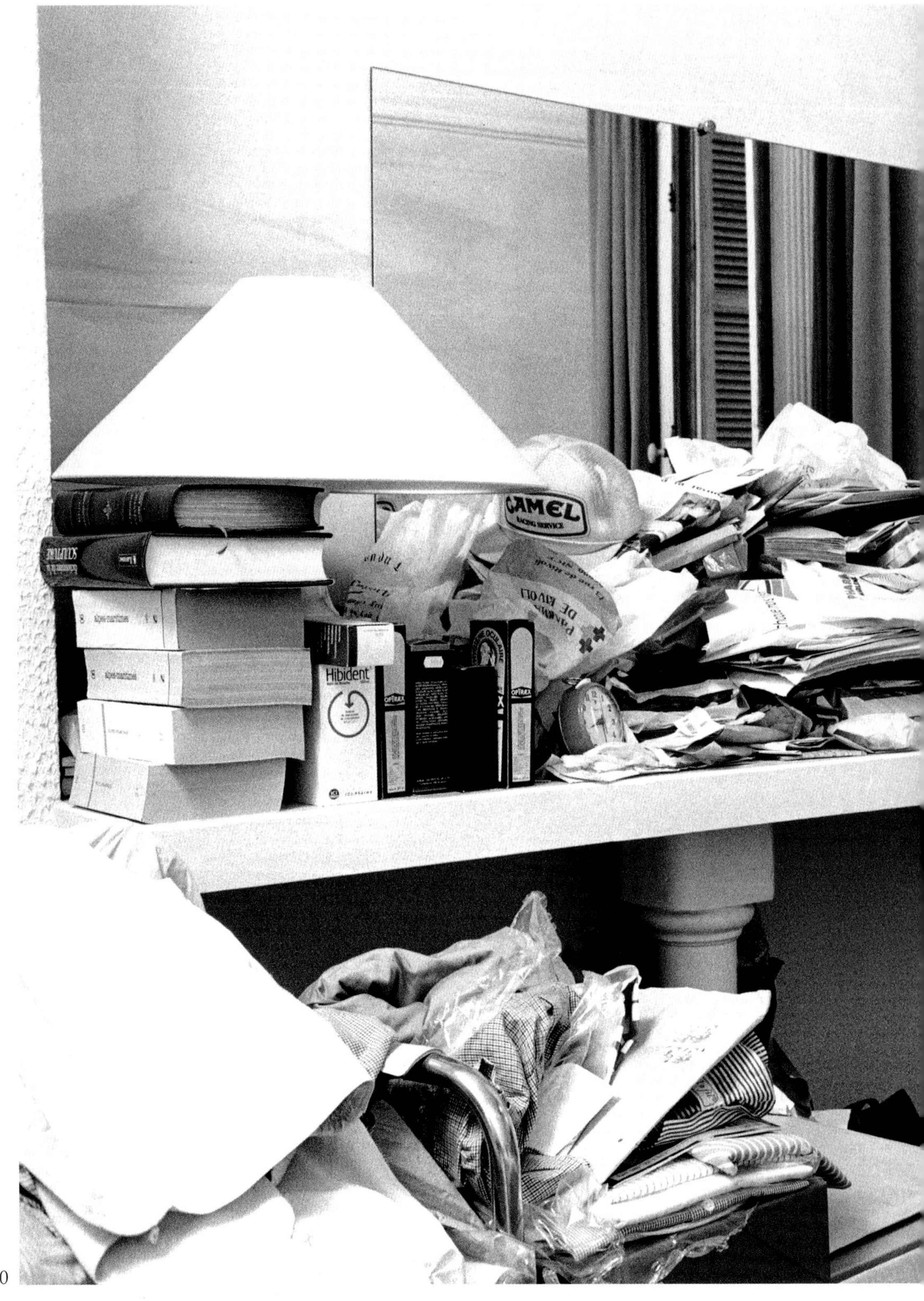
CAMEL
RACING SERVICE
Hibident

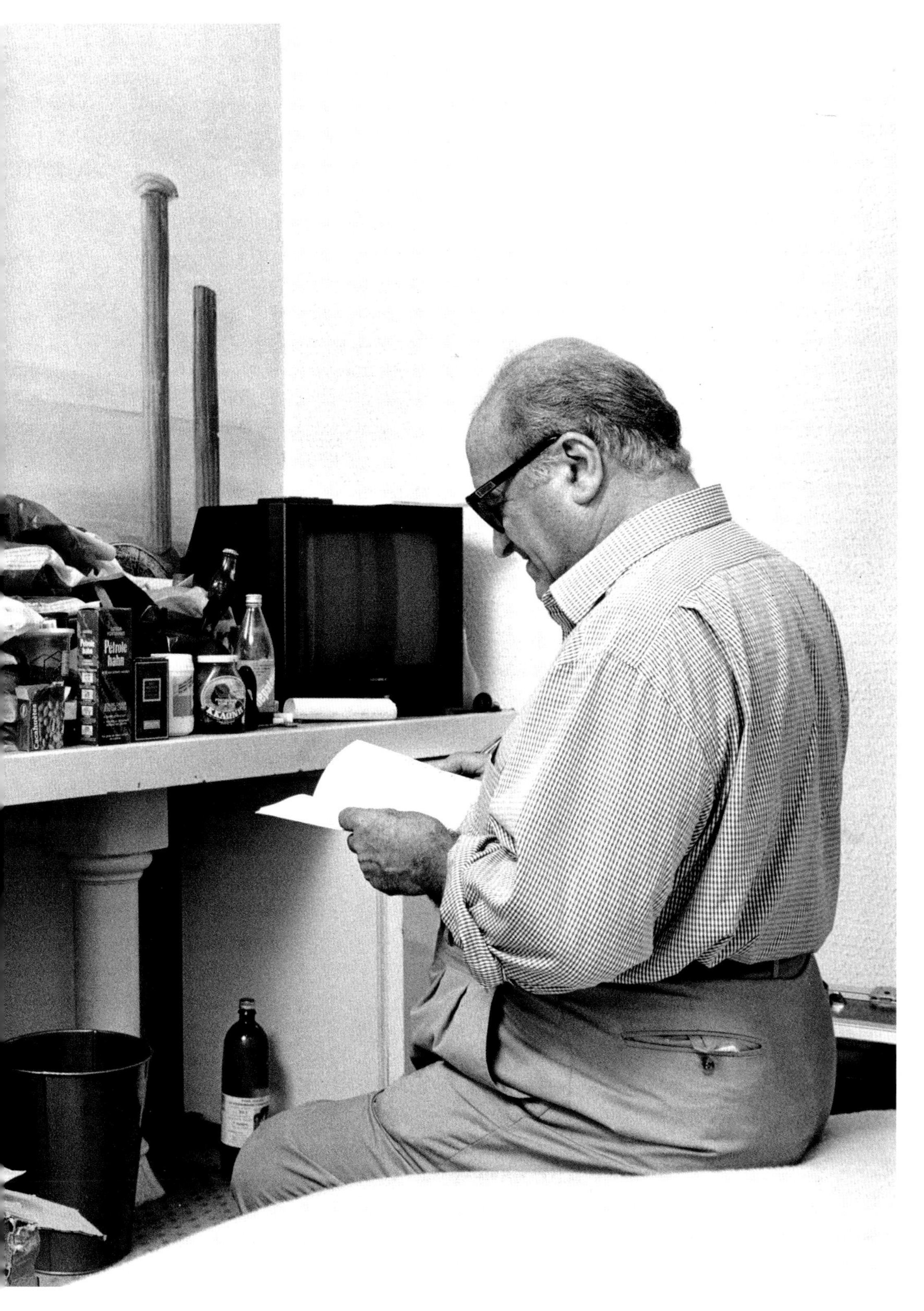
Pétrole
hahn

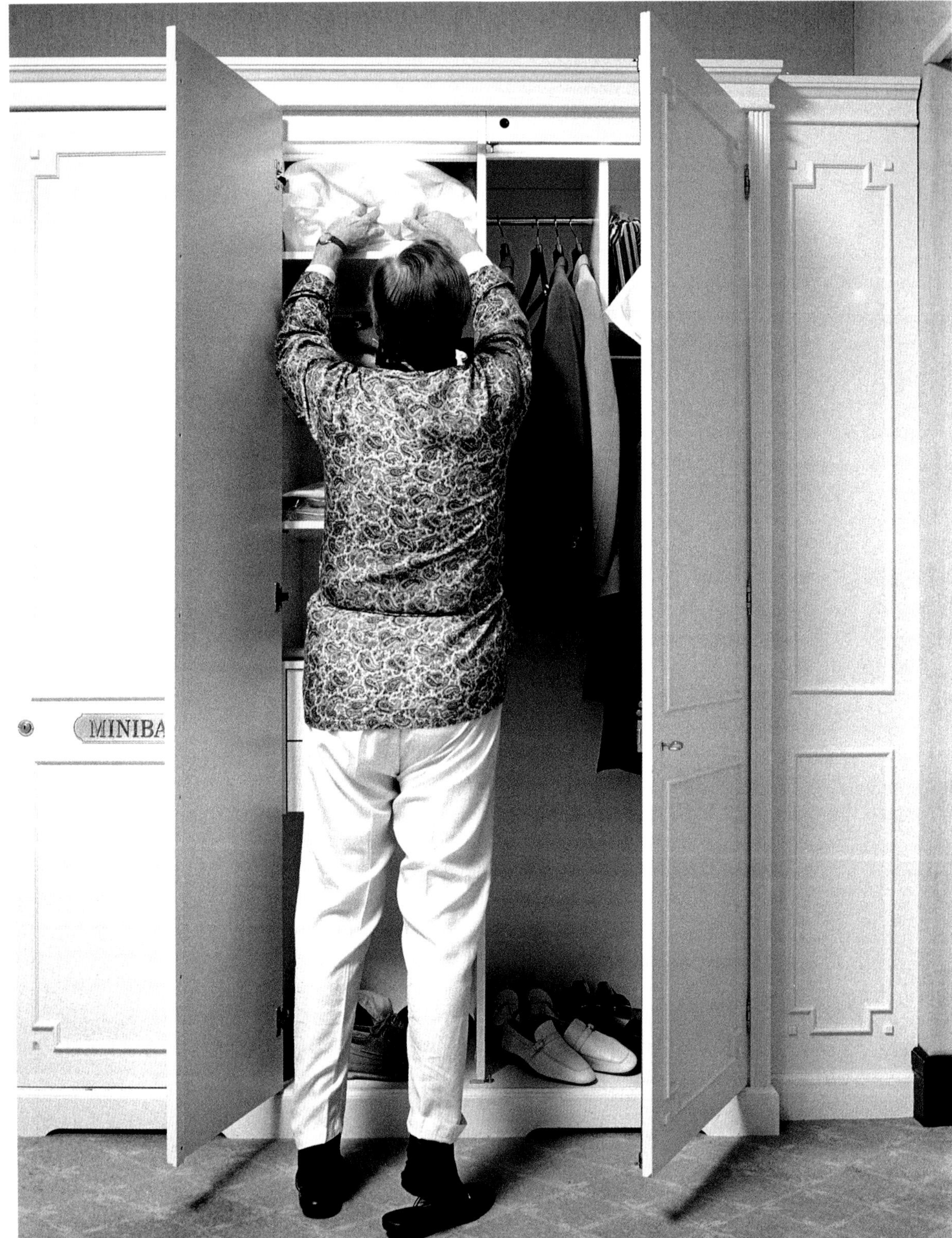
MINIBA

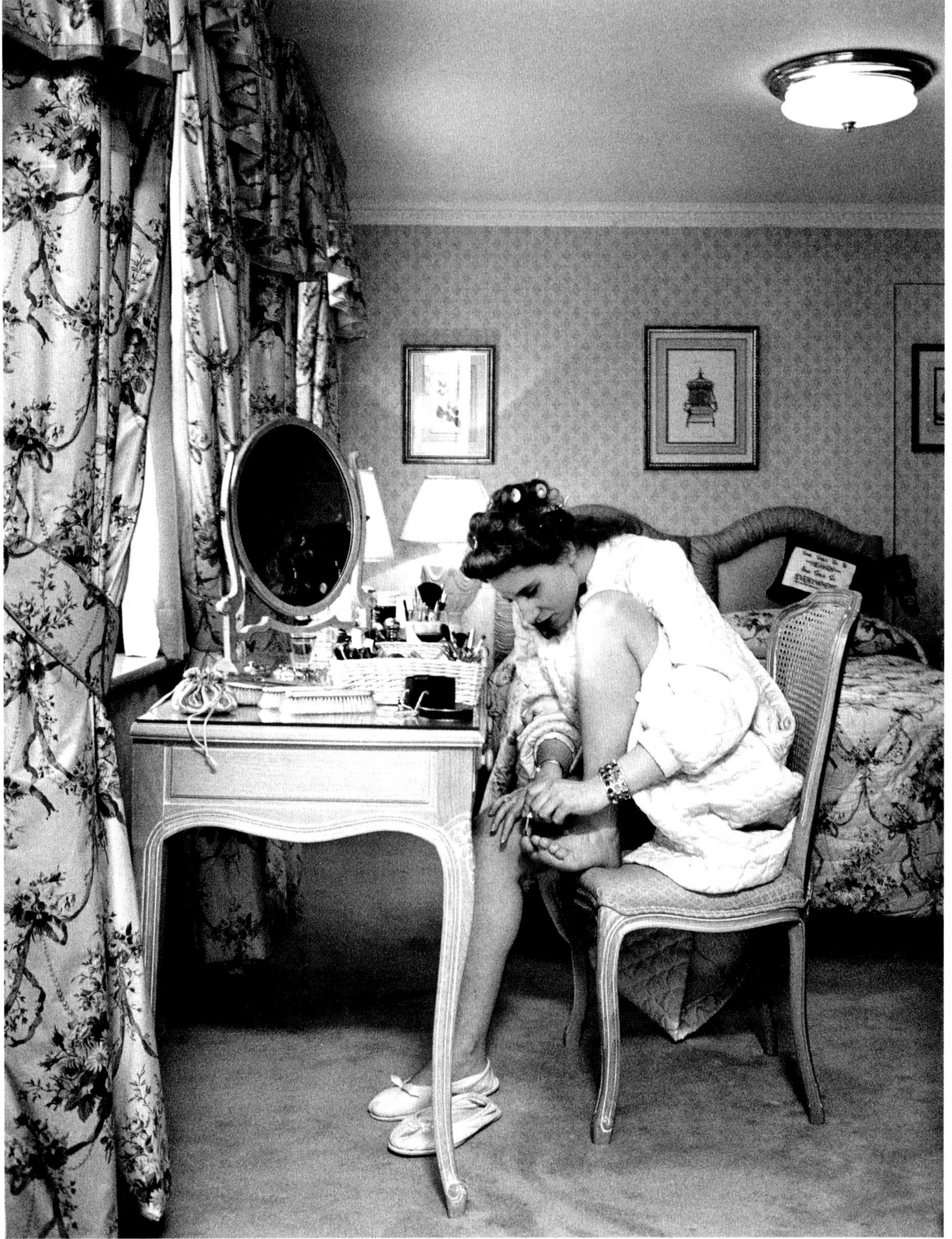

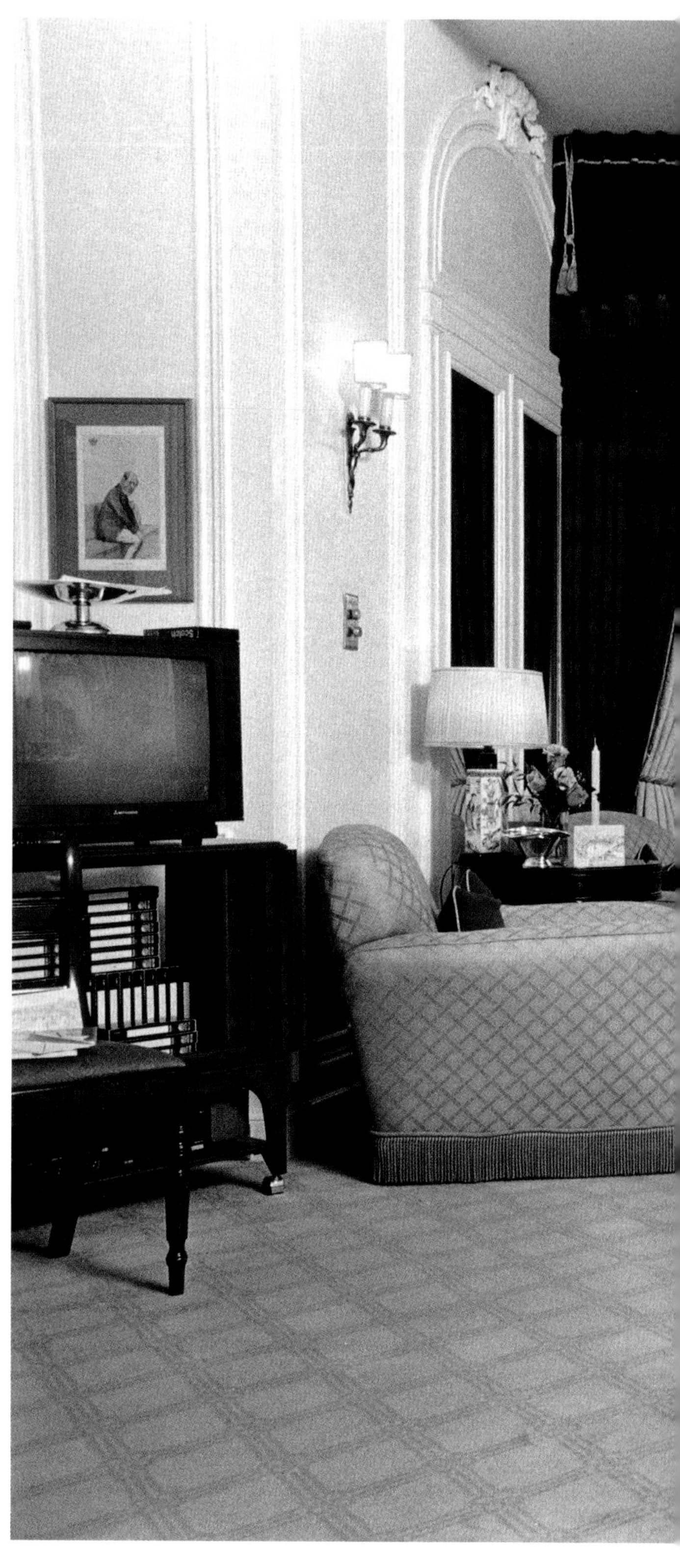

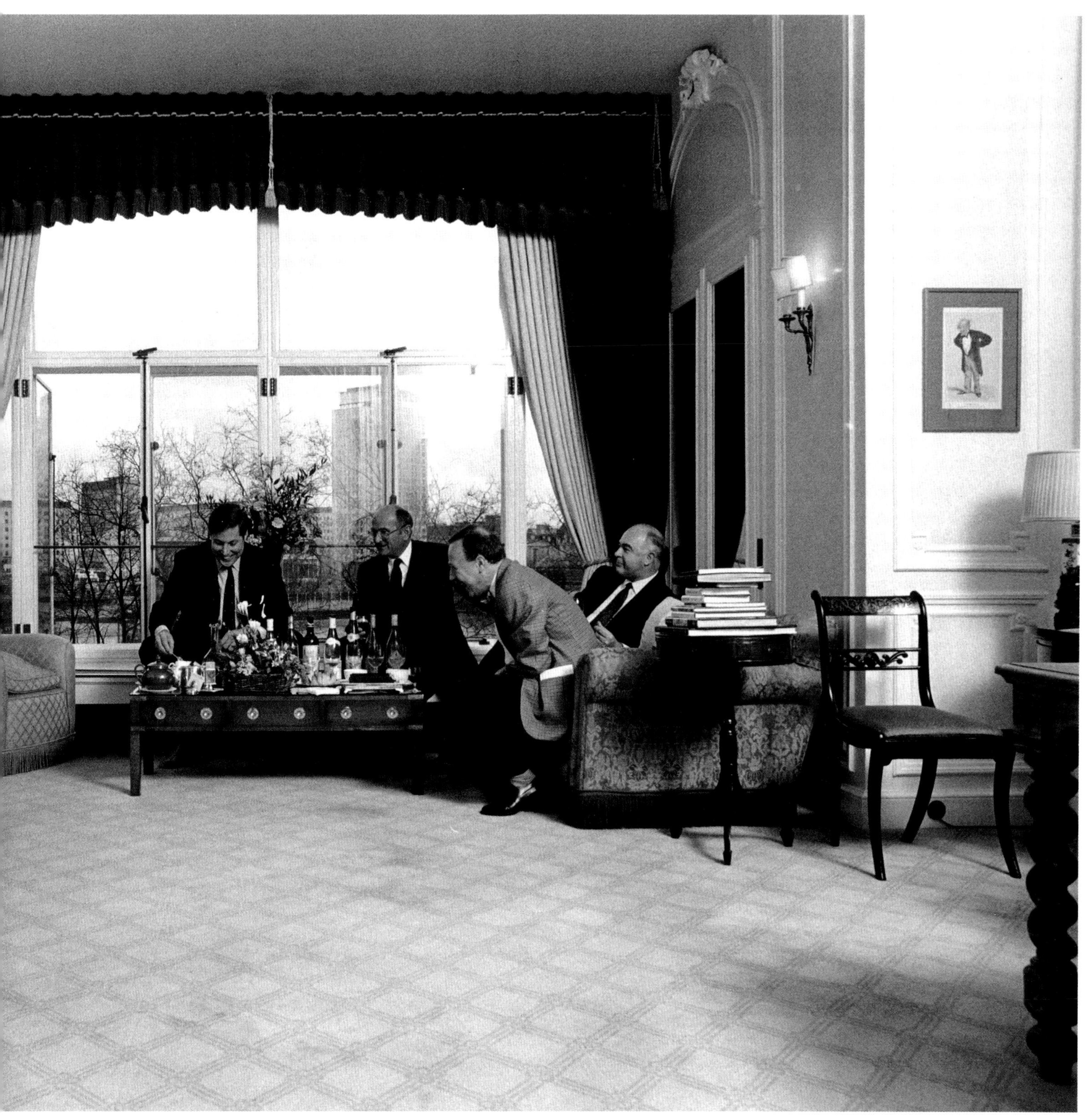

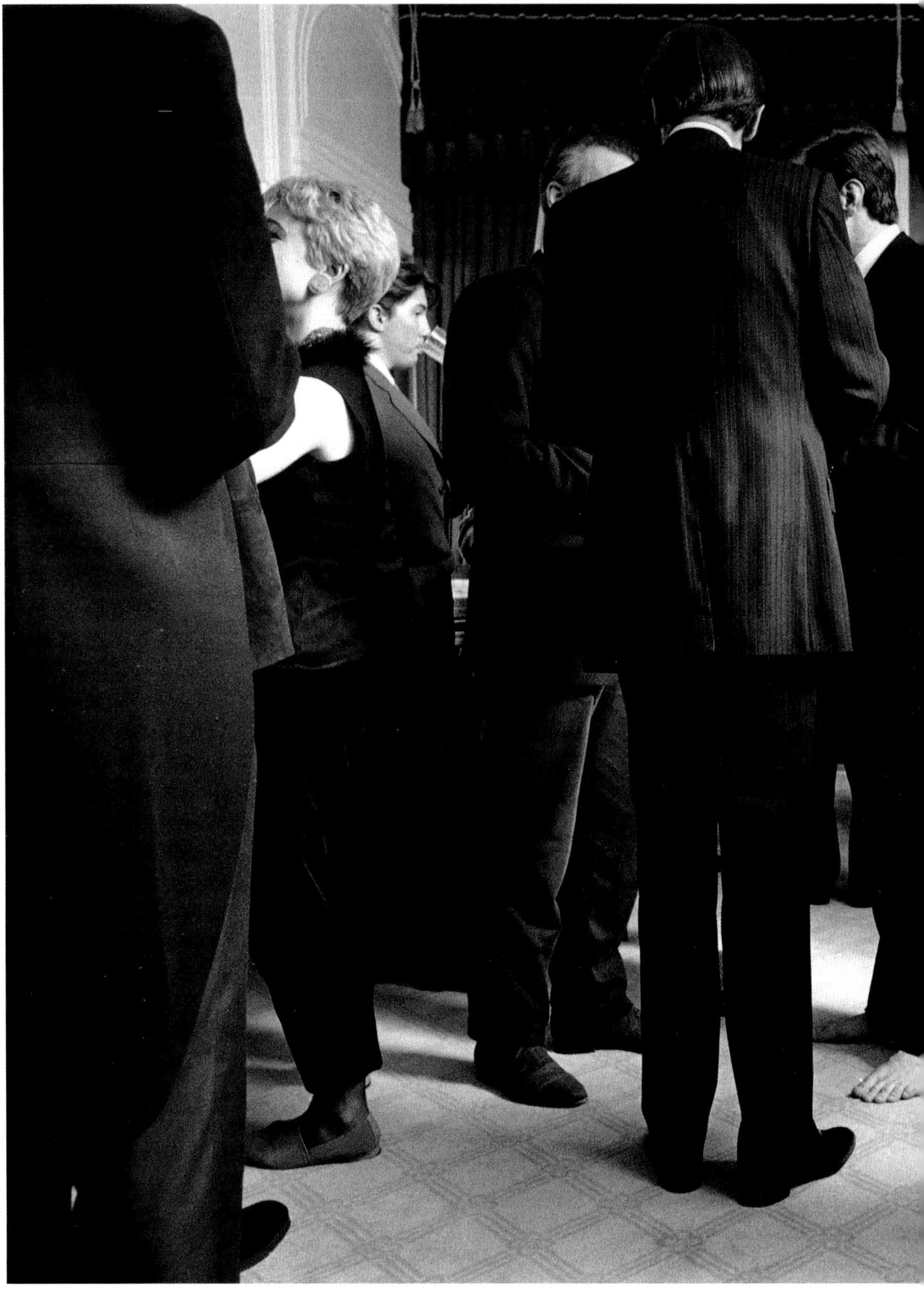

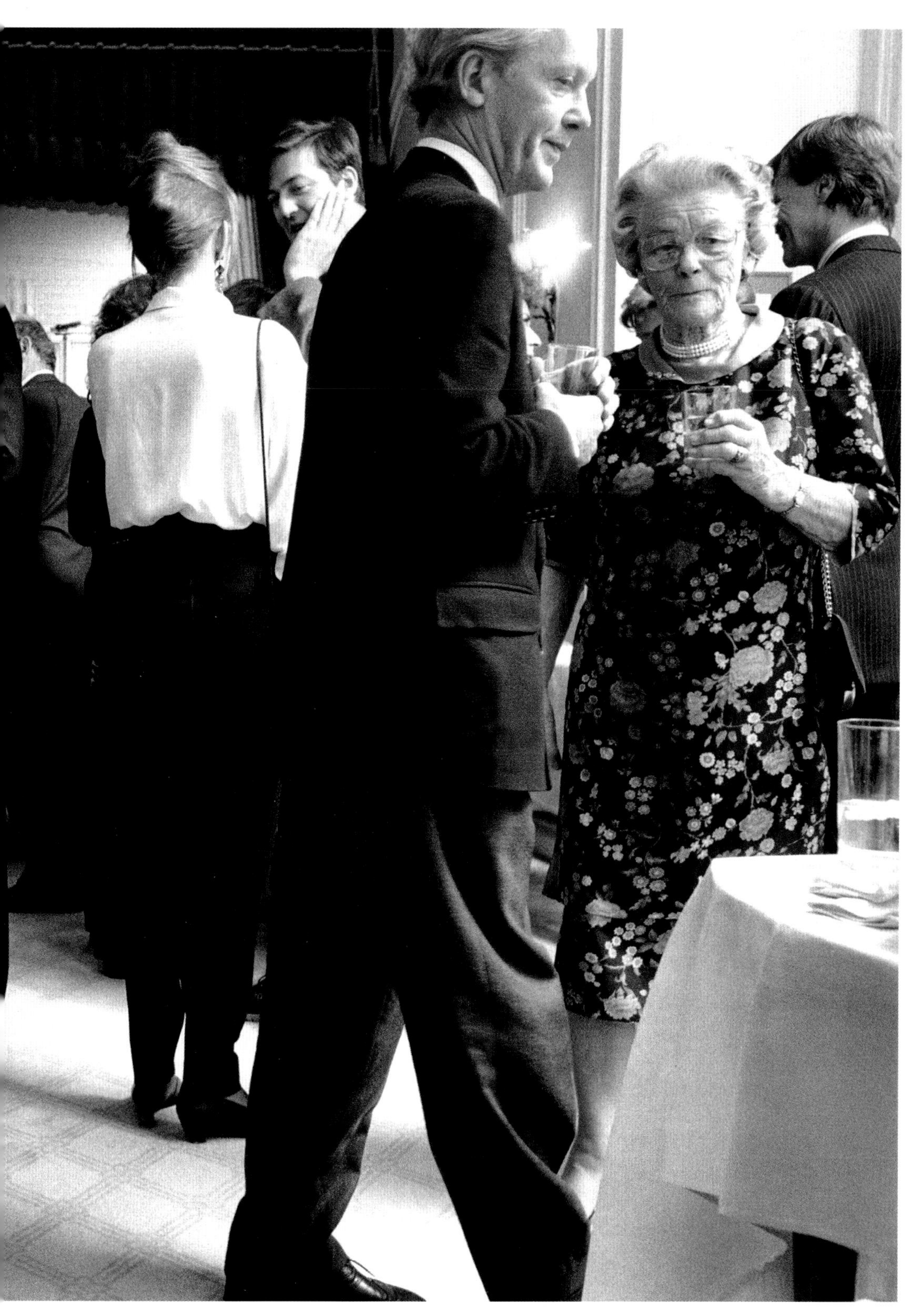

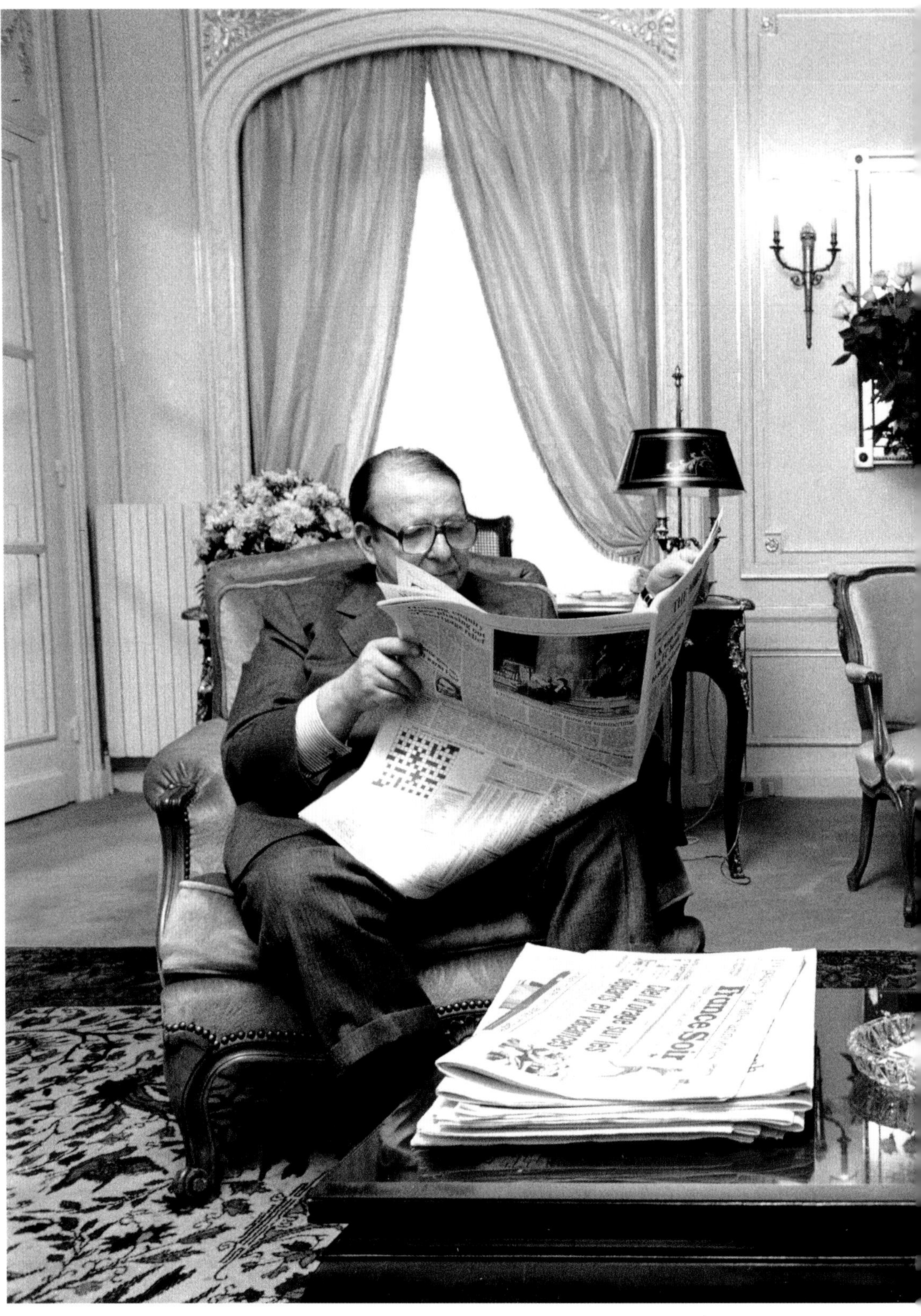
France Soir

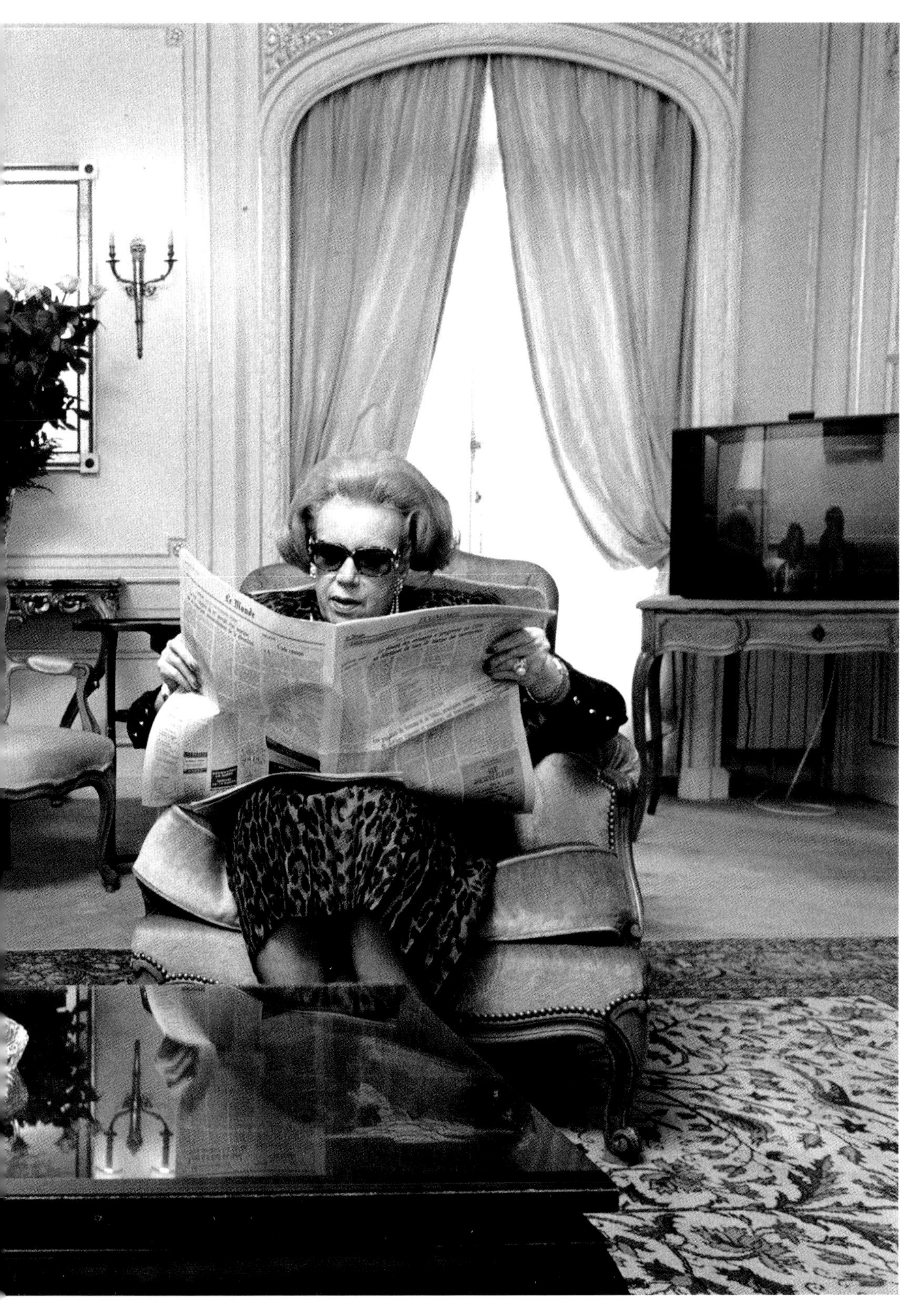
Le Monde

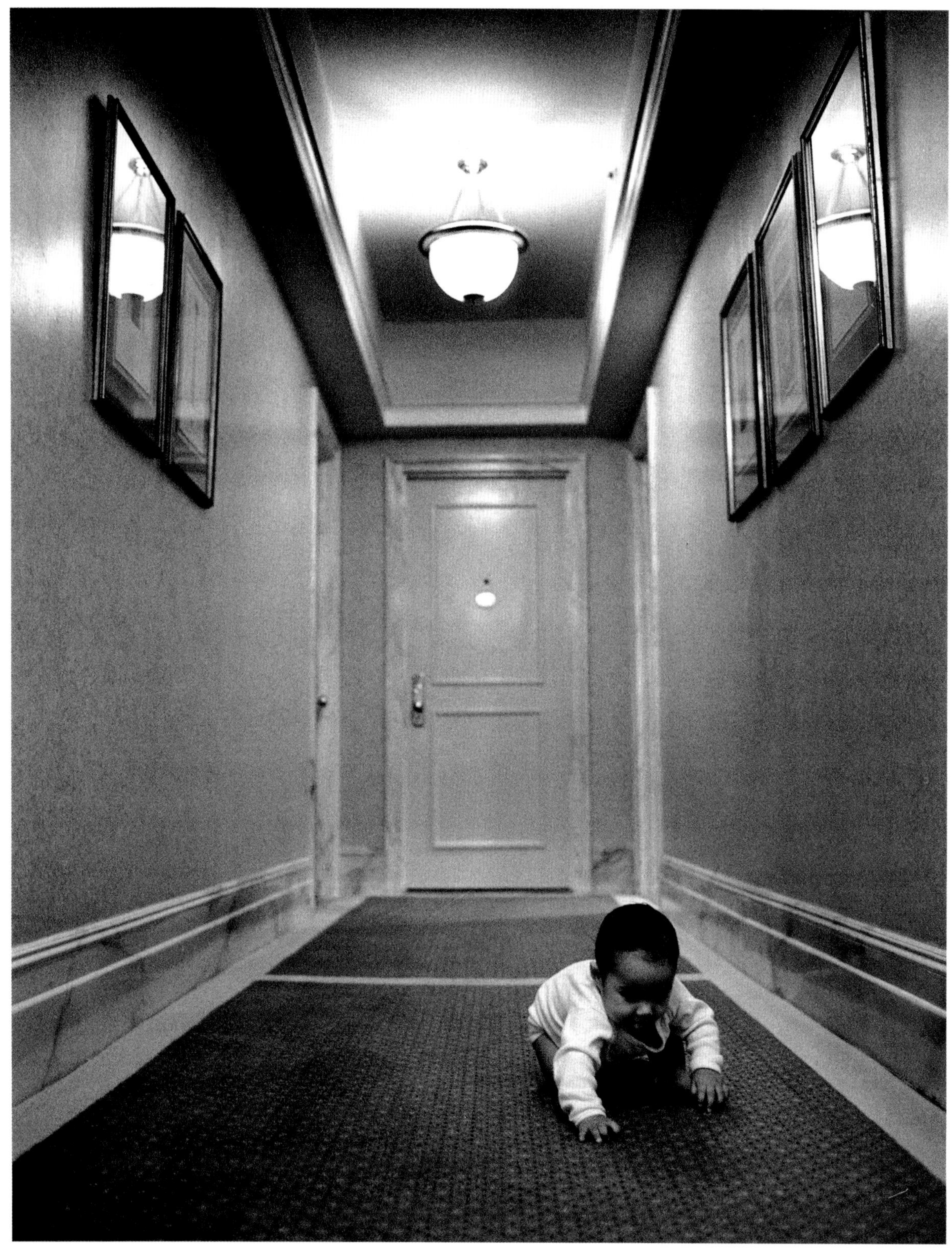

36

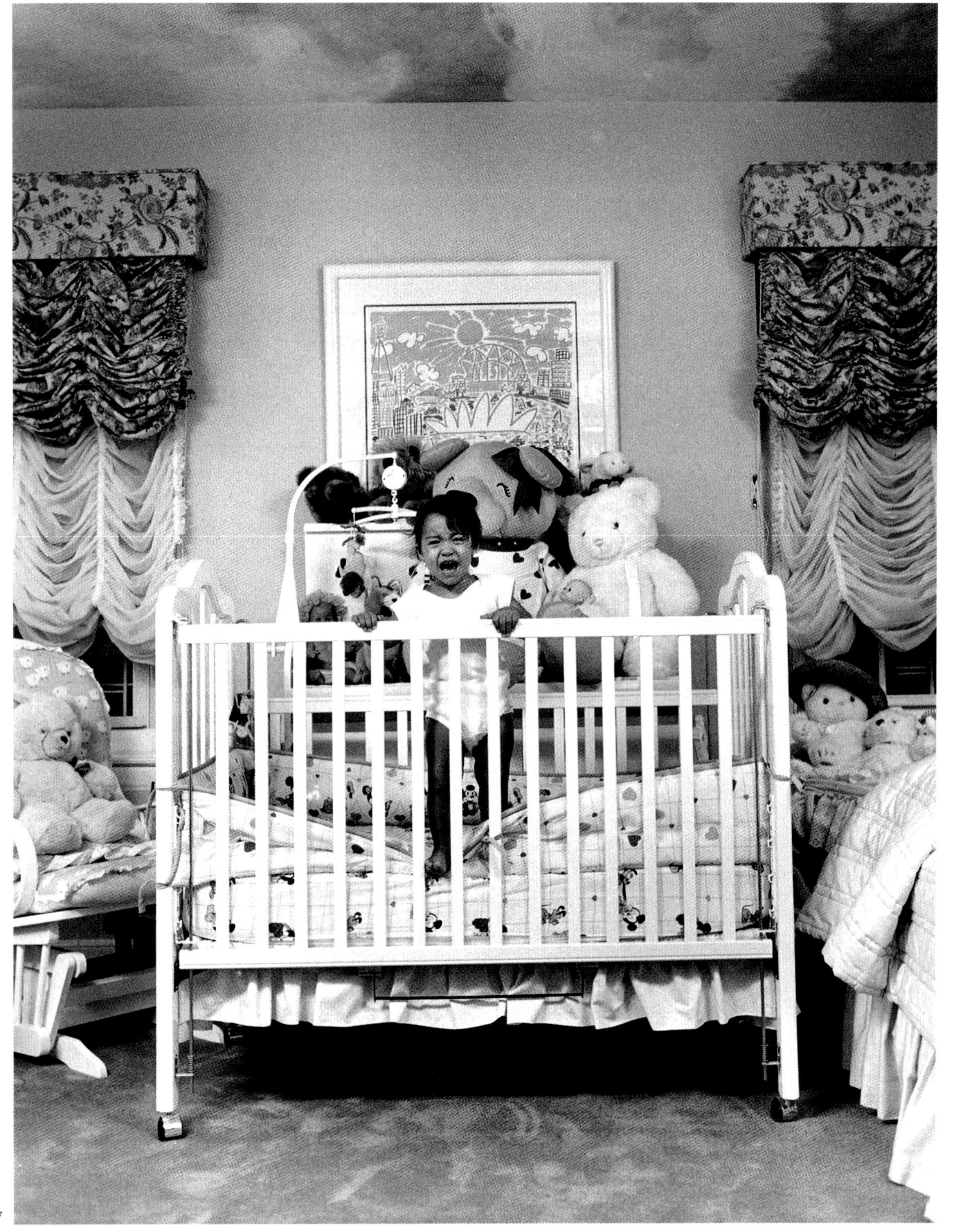

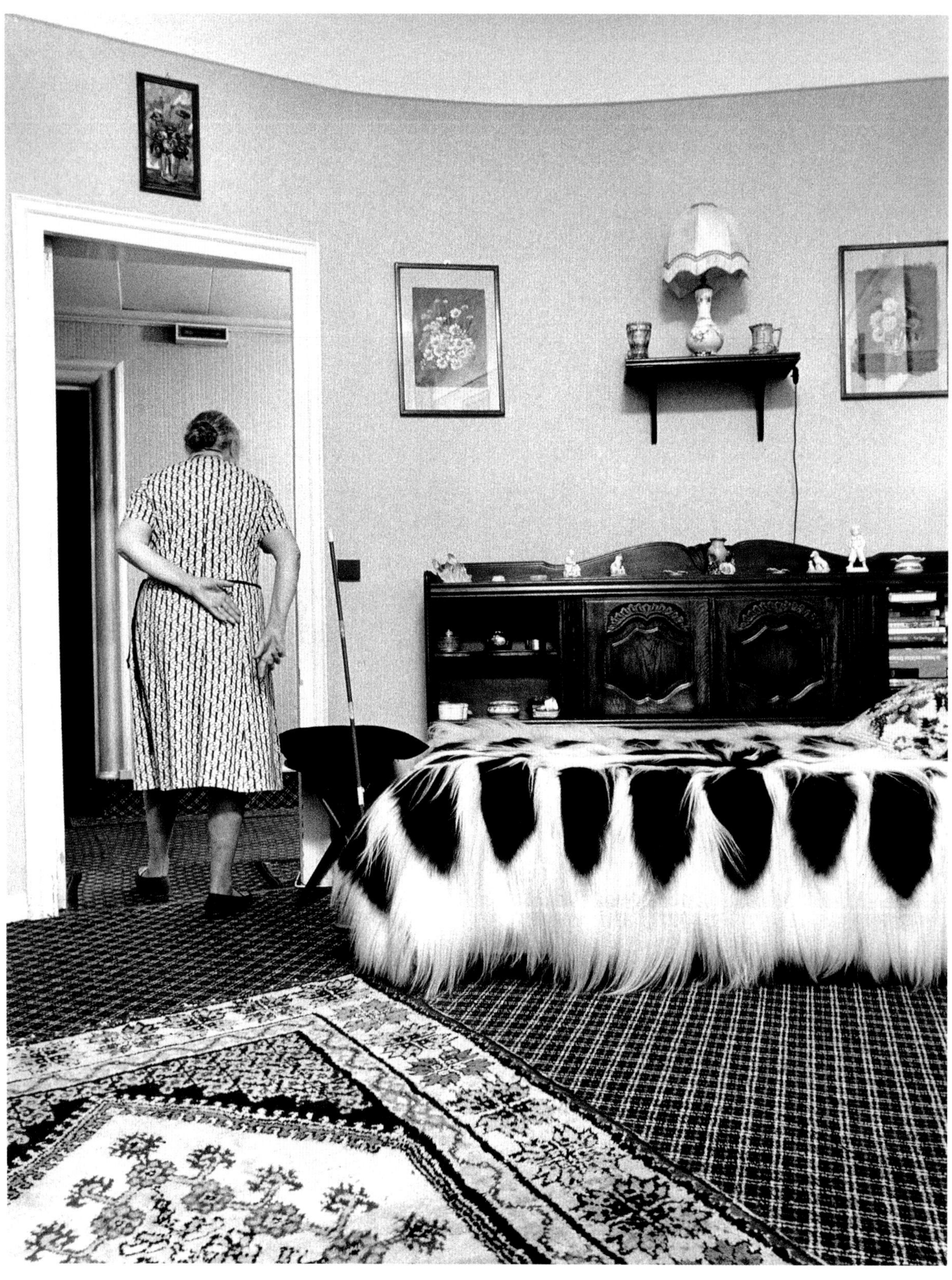